J.K. LASSE

NEW RULES FOR RETIREMENT AND TAX

Look for these and other titles from J.K. Lasser™—Practical Guides for All
Your Financial Needs

J.K. LASSER'S™

NEW RULES FOR RETIREMENT AND TAX

Paul Westbrook, CFP

John Wiley & Sons, Inc.
New York • Chichester • Weinheim • Brisbane • Singapore • Toronto

Published by John Wiley & Sons, Inc.
Published simultaneously in Canada.

This publication is designed to provide accurate and authoritative information in regard to the
subject matter covered. It is sold with the understanding that the publisher is not engaged in
rendering professional services. If professional advice or other expert assistance is required,
the services of a competent professional person should be sought.

ISBN 0-471-10475-2

Printed in the United States of America.

10 9 8 7 6 5 4 3 2 1

To Ashley, best wishes to discover the
very best possibilities of life.

To the thousands of people I've discussed this subject
with in seminars, and the hundreds of people
I've counseled individually. To them, I owe my insight
into this unique world called retirement.

Preface

Marilyn found me during a cocktail party after a speech I gave as part of a *Money* magazine conference in Boca Raton, Florida. She unloaded, "How can I plan? I'm about 15 to 20 years from retirement, recently divorced, don't have much of an investment nest egg. I'm in the middle." Her voice rose. "How can I determine where I am and how much I need to save?" She was the catalyst that shaped this book.

Because of time limits, I had focused my speech on only two critical groups needing retirement planning: younger people who need to think long term and older people at the cusp of retirement who need immediate help. Marilyn and many like her were left out, although mid-career people need just as much serious planning as anyone else. Also ignored were those who had already retired. They still need help too.

Marilyn's intensity caught me off guard. She was right to feel frustrated and surely represented many who would not express themselves so bluntly. This experience erased any doubt in my mind of the powerful influence retirement has over people's lives. By the time my plane touched down at Newark, I had resolved to do something about it.

First, I faxed Marilyn a worksheet guide for those in the middle. It was as straightforward and easy to use as the ones I had presented in Boca Raton. "Thanks," she responded, "that's exactly what I need."

Then I resolved to write the book I had been thinking about—a complete retirement book that would not leave anyone or any subject out. It had to include reliable planning guides at each of four critical times in people's lives. It had to provide a complete discussion of investments, a crucial key to retirement. It needed to cover Social Security, life expectancy, generations, and careers. It also needed to delve into why people are so preoccupied with retirement today.

In case you've been too busy to notice, 98 percent of us appear to be chasing retirement. At times thoughtfully, at times tediously, at times desperately, we are all marching arm-in-arm toward that holy grail of our workaday world: Retirement. It has even led me to refer to it as "Chasing the Big R."

And so I thank Marilyn, and all the others who have inspired me to write this book. Although I have been able to help many people with retirement planning over the years, I cannot meet and work with everyone seeking financial guidance. This book is for you. I hope it will help you, too. If it does, you can thank Marilyn, the blunt, urgently seeking-retirement catalyst from Boca Raton.

Acknowledgments

To Bill Arnone and Larry McCoombe for their wisdom and anecdotes, and especially their camaraderie.

To Mary Ann Foster for reviewing the entire manuscript and offering numerous valuable suggestions.

To others who have helped in different ways: Jesse Birnbaum, Jeremy Gold, Karin Halperin, Al Silverman, Rose Marie Stock, Anique Taylor, and Brigitte Weeks.

Finally, I want to thank Debra Englander, Executive Editor (at John Wiley & Sons), and David Pugh, Editor, who were most helpful in making the book better.

Contents

Summary of New Tax Law Highlights for Retirement

Individual Tax Rates

- Tax rebates in 2001 of up to $300 for singles and up to $600 for married.
- Rates to decline in steps:

2000	2001	2002	2006
39.6%	39.1%	38.6%	35%
36	35.5	35	33
31	30.5	30	28
28	27.5	27	25
15	refund credit	10–15	10–15

Retirement Contribution Limits (see Chapter 4)

- 2002 *IRA* contribution limits increased to $3,000 a year, and for those 50 and over an additional $500.

  Contribution limits increase to $5,000 by 2008, and additional amounts for those 50 and over increase to $1,000 starting in 2006.

- 2002 *401(k), 403(b), and 457* contribution limits increased to $11,000 a year, and for those 50 and over an additional $1,000.

Contribution limits gradually rise to $15,000 by 2006, and additional amounts for those 50 and over gradually rises to $5,000 by 2006.

- 2002 *SIMPLE* plan contribution limits are increased to $7,000 a year, and for those 50 and over an additional $500.

  Contribution limits are increased to $10,000 by 2005, and additional amounts for those 50 and over are increased to $2,500 by 2006.

- 2002 *SEP and Profit-Sharing* plan contribution dollar limits increased to $30,000 a year.

- 2002 *Money Purchase* plan contribution dollar limit increased to $35,000 a year.

Temporary Retirement Savings Tax Credit (see Chapter 4)

- Beginning in 2002, and through 2006, a tax credit is available up to $1,000 for those contributing to a regular IRA, Roth IRA, 401(k), 403(b), 457, SEP, or SIMPLE plan. If married, you must earn $50,000 or less; if head of household, you must earn $37,500 or less; and if single or married filing separately, you must earn $25,000 or less.

Deemed IRA (see Chapter 4)

- Beginning in 2003, organizations can set up IRAs, such as a 401(k) plan, as part of their savings plan.

Increased Rollover Flexibility (see Chapters 4 and 14)

- Beginning in 2002, all 401(k), 403(b), and 457 plans can be rolled over into an IRA (including after-tax amounts), or directly into each other, if the plan allows it.

- Beginning in 2002, a surviving spouse can roll over a deceased spouse's 401(k), 403(b), or 457 plan into his or her 401(k), 403(b), or 457 plan, if the plan allows it.

Estate Taxes (see Chapter 16)

- **Increased exclusion**

2002	$1 million
2004	$1.5 million
2006	$2 million
2009	$3.5 million

- **Decreased rates**

  2002   Top rate is 50 percent

  2003–2007   Top rate is reduced 1 percent per year to 45 percent

- **Estate tax (and generation-skipping tax) eliminated—2010**

- **Need for Congress to renew—2011**

Other Recent Retirement Tax and Law Highlights

- 2001 New simpler 70½ rules for IRA and benefit plans for minimum distributions, including new table (see Chapter 14).

- 2000 Elimination of Social Security earnings test at 65, or full retirement age (see Chapter 8).

- 2001–2002 Social Security earnings test for year 65, or full retirement, is $25,000 in 2001, $30,000 in 2002 (see Chapter 8).

CHAPTER 1

Chasing the Big R through Four Financial Steps

You can see it in the eyes of the 30-something GenX computer programmer absorbed in chat rooms seeking alternatives for crashed stock options. You can feel it in the heartbeat of the 40- or 50-something baby boomer marketing specialist who desperately hopes to quit the rat race. You can detect it in the worn face of the 60-something lawyer who can't wait to end the commute. Everyone wants it. Retirement.

The power of retirement is enormous. It has become our national pastime. Articles about it are everywhere. People discuss it over lunch, at barbecues, and at coffee machines. They click on the more than nine hundred Web sites that provide retirement calculators. People contemplate retirement in their quiet time after a frustrating workday. Retirement. I call it the *Big R*.

Many workers, however, feel like frustrated lab rats who can't find the end of the maze or gerbils who can't run fast enough on the revolving wheel. That our parents attained financial security by working and saving patiently year after year is too slow for the twenty-first century.

I was in an elevator with an armful of retirement seminar books when a young man, about 20, said, "Retirement, that's great." I asked him why he was interested in retirement at such a young age. "Oh, I intend to retire early." I asked him just how early. "Oh, probably not until about 35."

Why this obsession? On the surface, it's obvious: Retirement represents the ultimate—not working and having enough money to live comfortably. Or as retirees have been telling me for 20 years, "The time when I can do what I want, when I want, and how I want." That's compelling.

Yet, all this obsessing suggests that there is something deeper here: Perhaps people are chasing an ideal life more than actual "retirement." This idea is explored in Chapter 11. But for now, let's zero in on your number one question about retirement: "How can I get it?" This is the heart of the book.

A major problem with retirement articles and books is that they're either too simple or (and this is more common) too complicated. The simple version is blunt: "You'll need 75 percent of your income." This is not very helpful. In fact, it's just about useless without making other assumptions.

The overly complex version isn't much help either. It is what many mutual funds have waiting for you: twenty pages of interminable calculations. Just as Einstein, after unraveling endless mathematics, revealed that simple and profound conclusion $E = MC^2$, you may successfully complete your retirement equation. After 20 pages, however, you are not only exhausted, you're still not sure whether you can retire. Your intuition warns that if just one of those numbers or calculations is wrong, your house of cards falls.

The Four Financial Steps

So, let's strike a balance. Instead of using one unwieldy table or worksheet for everyone at any age, which makes it too complicated for everyone, I have broken planning down into four bite-sized financial steps and worksheets:

Step 1. If you're early in your career and retirement is a hazy far-off dream, you must concentrate on getting a solid savings and investment plan in place.

Step 2. If you're in mid-career, when you have to juggle many priorities besides retirement, you need help in creating a glide path to retirement.

Step 3. If you're at retirement's door, it is time to double-check your plan to make sure everything is in order.

Step 4.   If you're already in retirement, the suggestions in this book can help
you stay financially afloat.

How to Use This Book

You can approach this book from several directions. You can start at the specific financial chapter that applies to your situation. There are four choices:

Step 1.   If you're in your 20s and 30s, start with Chapter 2.

Step 2.   If you're in your 40s and 50s, read Chapter 6 first.

Step 3.   If you're at the cusp of retirement, turn to Chapter 13.

Step 4.   If you're in retirement, look at Chapter 15.

Or, you can start with a subject that focuses on one of your burning financial concerns, such as retirement on a shoestring (Chapter 12), investments
(Chapter 3), help with the discipline of saving money or getting out of
debt (Chapter 4), or the handling of IRA rollovers and other technical stuff
(Chapter 14).

Or, you can simply turn to a chapter that offers a different slant on a subject
you thought you knew, such as careers (Chapter 5), the future of Social Security (Chapter 8), life expectancy (Chapter 9), generations and why people retire (Chapter 11). Simply search for chapters that you'd like to explore.

If you want to reference tax information such as 401(k), 403(b), 457 plans,
Keoghs, and IRAs, Chapter 4 reviews how much you can contribute; Chapter 5
reviews rollovers when you change jobs; Chapter 14 reviews distributions when
you retire, including the new rules at 70½ for benefit plans and IRAs; and Chapter 16 reviews distributions if you are a beneficiary.

If you want a touch of some heavy-duty technical stuff, the *Honors Section* is
at the end of Chapter 2. You can, and probably will, ignore it. That's okay. It is
there for those who want to delve deeper into such retirement concepts as how
replacement ratios and future values are calculated and what the Monte Carlo
technique tries to accomplish. It won't change your retirement planning, but it
can give a better understanding of the technical issues of retirement.

Finally, those of you who want to find out how it all ends might just jump to
the last chapter—Chapter 17, The Chase Is Over: How You Can Enjoy Retirement Once There.

The Stories of Liz and Harold

RETIREMENT IS NOT EASY OR AUTOMATIC. ASK LIZ AND HAROLD.

Liz, 57, worked for a major corporation. During a retirement seminar, she volunteered that retirement scared her to death. She even hated the idea of it because she loved her work and most of her friends were at the company. She was single, without children, and her job was the central stabilizing aspect of her life. A few years later, when she was forced to retire, she had to go through the slow and difficult process of developing a personal life. How did she do it? Being forced to do something, because she was a naturally busy person, she gave in at first to simple everyday activities like calling friends already retired and family members to say hello. Then she heard that her library needed volunteers, so she signed up. A year or two later when I ran into her, I asked her if she was still missing the office. She looked surprised and laughed, "You know, I'd never thought I would say it, but now, I'll never go back."

Harold, 72, works for a prestigious department store in Westchester, just north of New York City. He is the most energetic salesperson in the store. "I've found myself again. I'd worked all my life as a middle manager in a company, got a good pension plus Social Security, and was happy the day I retired. But soon I began to feel that my life was becoming meaningless. I didn't want to volunteer at the hospital, couldn't find a hobby, and I just got in my wife's way at home. Now that I'm working again I feel like I did years ago—full of energy and life."

Step by step, chapter by chapter, you'll be able to see your retirement plan emerge as your numbers and thoughts merge into a plan that makes sense to you.

Retirement: The Most Complex of All Financial Objectives

Some money objectives are simple to calculate, although they may be difficult to attain. Buying a house requires a down payment, which is easy enough to determine. It's also easy to calculate the cost of four years of college. Saving enough to cover it, is another matter.

Retirement is like constructing the Empire State building versus putting up a pup tent. How should you invest your 401(k) or other plans? How will the stock market do? How much should you be saving? Will you have pensions, and what annuity form should you take, or if offered, should you take a lump sum? Is Social Security really sound and should you take it at 62 or 65? How long will you live (which could be 30 or more years after you retire)? What will inflation do to your money over that time? Should you take out long-term care insurance?

How do you even start to deal with something as complex as retirement? Sit down, take a deep breath, and take it piece by piece. A good place to start is with the simple idea of a retirement envelope.

The Retirement Envelope

Retirement is a balancing act—your retirement expenses balanced by enough financial resources. That's all retirement requires: You must have enough money to afford your year-by-year living expenses. You knew that. Sometimes, though, you can get lost in the details of planning your retirement. A diagram called the *retirement envelope* provides this overview visually (see Figure 1.1).

The envelope, like other planning diagrams that defines the parameters of a problem, defines the retirement problem. The horizontal line is your time line, moving from left to right, with R the point of retirement. This is age 55, 62, or

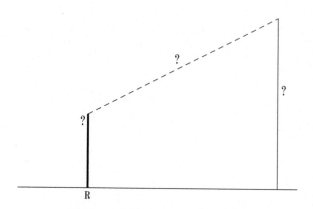

FIGURE 1.1 Basic retirement envelope.

whatever date you have tentatively chosen. Then, there are three critical parameters, or questions:

1. What are your first year's retirement expenses? The vertical line directly above the R represents this. It's the amount of money needed for your first year in retirement. For your neighbor, it could be $32,000; for you, it may be $55,000. How to estimate this is explained in Chapter 6.

2. How will your expenses increase with inflation during retirement? The upward sloping dotted line represents this. Should you estimate inflation at 2 percent? 5 percent? In Chapter 7, I talk about inflation for everyone, not just the boomers, and how to estimate it for your retirement.

3. How many retirement years should you plan for? This is represented by the last vertical line which shows hypothetically how long you'll live. We don't know how long we'll actually live (and perhaps we wouldn't want to know even if we could), but you'll learn how to estimate it for your planning in Chapter 9.

Although this envelope is a generalized look at retirement, as you go through the book you'll be able to answer each of these questions for yourself and then can sketch your own envelope. It will help you visualize when you have enough resources through income streams (e.g., pensions and Social Security) and investments (e.g., 401(k)s, IRAs, and savings) to fill up your envelope. That's when you'll have enough to retire.

Your envelope may look like the one in Figure 1.2.

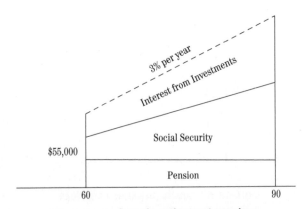

FIGURE 1.2 Sample retirement envelope.

The History of Retirement in a Minute and a Half

Retirement began in 1940, when Ida Mae Fuller, a Vermont bookkeeper, became the first person to draw money from Social Security. Because retirement jumps so easily to mind, it's hard to think of it as a relatively new idea.

Before 1940, most people simply worked all their lives. Through our distant agrarian and mercantile past, the Industrial Revolution, and up through the Great Depression of the 1930s, retirement essentially did not exist. The Depression forced a significant change.

In 1935, Social Security was put into place as a response to a prolonged and devastating 25 percent level of unemployment. For the first time, older people were guaranteed a base, a modest guaranteed income, so they could retire and make room for younger people who needed to be employed. Ironically, when Ida received that first Social Security check, we were on the verge of World War II and the economy was finally starting to grow. But Social Security was firmly in place, and it created the practicality of universal retirement.

Then pensions followed. Before World War II, pensions had been a rarity. When wages were frozen during the war, companies created and increased benefits including some pensions to attract and hold employees. After the war, companies sensed that pensions could be a significant employment incentive and set actuaries to work designing them for nonunion as well as union workers. Returning military personnel appreciated the future security held out by their own individual pensions.

When people had some extra money from the booming postwar economy, they started to save. All the pieces were now in place. Social Security, pensions, and savings. It was even dubbed the three-legged retirement stool. Today, happily, 30 million Idas, or one-tenth of our country's citizens, are retired. By 2031 when my daughter will be 50, there will be over twice as many—70 million, or one-fifth of the U.S. population.

Why Are Pensions Disappearing?

But retirement, alas, doesn't stand still. Pensions, one of the pillars of retirement of the 1950s through the 1980s, have been performing an amazing shrinking act. In the late 1970s, at their peak of popularity, almost half of all workers had pensions. Now barely one in four has them. What happened?

First, as pensions became more popular, governmental regulations became more complex, and finally burdensome. Small- and medium-size companies found them too costly to maintain and discarded their plans. Second, to save money, large companies morphed their pensions into new scaled-down versions called cash balance plans. As many as one-third of large companies have already converted to these newer plans or are in the process of doing so.

For older workers, converting from pensions to cash balance plans usually means a frozen benefit with no additional pension credits. But, other than the recent furor at IBM, workers' protests have lacked support; more commonly, workers underestimate their pensions' worth.

Consider the case of an executive named Jeanne. She came to me for help in evaluating the worth of her traditional pension plan. She was considering a job opportunity outside her company. The potential job wasn't an opportunity to die for, but she was exploring her options. She was 52 years old and had been with her company for 25 years. Her question was: What would be the financial impact if she left before she was entitled to her age 55 pension?

She was in a sensitive job and didn't want to publicize her job exploration, so she asked me, instead of her benefits department, to calculate her pension. In three years, she would be able to retire with an annual pension of $42,000. (Age 55 is often a magic number for pensions.) Leaving her company before then would cut her age 55 pension one-third to $28,000. If she stayed, she would have critical medical insurance coverage for the rest of her life as well as her more lucrative pension. She didn't have trouble understanding my advice. I recommended that she think seriously of staying because of the significant financial loss she would incur. This was also dependent on her feeling confident that her job would not be eliminated during the next three years. Jeanne decided to stay at her company, delaying her search for a new job.

But for younger corporate workers, cash balance plans are just fine. As with 401(k) plans, cash balance plans allow workers to see how much they have in the plan, their "balance," which they could take if they left the firm. Although the balances only grow by a modest fixed amount each year, the company makes all the contributions, so it's found money.

Then, too, this points out one of the differences inherent between generations. You can hear it from an old-timer, just turning 65, reminiscing about having worked 40 years with the same company and complaining that he is the last of a breed: "No one wants to work for the same company anymore." Indeed, few, if any, younger workers will ever want to think in those terms. But cash balance plans are portable, ideal for younger workers who think in terms of an astounding 10 to 12 different jobs before they retire. Traditional pensions have virtually no meaning here.

The concept of generations, a useful if imprecise concept, has given me the ability to better understand other changes occurring in retirement, besides pensions. It explains how a spectrum of birth years lodged in a particular historical time creates certain values and expectations affecting attitudes about money and retirement. People of different ages do have different ideas. In fact, retirement itself is tailored to each generation, a concept that is explored in Chapter 11.

A Definition of Retirement

I have often talked to people who have left a long-term job, or received a pension, but continue to work. When they tell me they are "retired," I ask them how they can be retired if they are still working. They are always at a loss in answering me. This is common with those in the armed services, police, and fire departments. They often retire after 20 years with a pension, even when the amount is not enough to fully retire from employment. They say they are retired, but they are still working. One man at a seminar told me he was retiring for the third time.

So, what is retirement? Here is my definition of retirement: when you don't have to work, because you have enough money for the rest of your life.

Why is this definition important? Because it defines retirement as that point at which you reach financial independence. You are then free to work or not. You can volunteer at the hospital, pursue a hobby, spend time with your grandchildren, or continue to work.

> **DEFINITION**
>
> **RETIREMENT**
> When you don't have to work, because you have enough money for the rest of your life.

This independence is the essence of today's retirement. It translates into the ability to determine what you want to do. And that makes all the difference in today's world.

On to the Chase

In the spirit of David Letterman, here are the top 10 reasons for the Chase:

10. In the world of work, you have nothing else to prove.
9. You don't like your boss.
8. You don't like your job.
7. The commute is getting to you.

6. You want to stop and smell the roses.

5. Retirement is a fad and you want in.

4. All your friends are retired.

3. You want to play hooky on all Mondays and Fridays.

2. All of the above.

And the number one reason?

1. You want to collect your reward.

Where is the best place to begin your chase? Start with the financial chapter that is most applicable to you: Chapter 2, 6, 13, or 15 (or even Chapter 12, which explains how to retire on a shoestring). Then, explore the other chapters to put your finances in the context of a total retirement plan. Chapter by chapter, step by step, your retirement plan will emerge.

I promise to avoid technical jargon wherever possible and to provide simplified, accurate tables that can assist you in assembling your plan.

So, let's join the chase.

CHAPTER 2

Step 1. Getting Started— Your 10-12-15 Percent Solution

You are young and you want a simple answer. You want to know how much you need to save to retire on time, so here it is:

The 10-12-15 Percent Solution

Age 25	Save 10 percent of your salary.
Age 30	Save 12 percent of your salary.
Age 40	Save 15 percent of your salary.

If you're just starting your career and are, say, between ages 20 and 25, *save 10 percent of your salary* until you retire. If you're 30 and haven't yet begun to put money away, *save 12 percent of your salary.* If you're 40 and have $50,000 in retirement investments, *save 15 percent of your salary.*

If you're 40 and have zero retirement savings, you'll either need to push back your plans for retirement or save a whopping 22 percent a year. If you're in this bind, however, you might need to resort to retiring on a shoestring (Chapter 12).

This 10-12-15 percent savings rate is the most important retirement action you can take early in your career. Simply start and continue a systematic savings and investment program. It will, in general, allow you to retire at age 65. It also allows for an emergency or two that requires you to dip into some of the money. Thus, it not only prescribes your retirement savings target, it allows you to have financial flexibility for life's uncertainties.

These calculations assume that you'll live to age 90 and that you'll enjoy a 25-year retirement. If you're married and your spouse also works and earns the same salary, then you'll have $2 million between you. The rates also assume there will be no employer match to your investments, like a 401(k) plan, and that you'll have no pensions. With any of these additions, your retirement will be more comfortable.

These rates do assume you'll receive a 3 percent salary increase each year and that you'll need about 65 percent of your then salary at retirement to maintain your lifestyle. If your salary grows faster, or slower, you'll still contribute 10 percent, 12 percent, or 15 percent of it to retirement investments. Lower taxes, no work expenses, and not having to save for retirement anymore are the prime reasons that explain the lower financial requirement of 65 percent. Later in this chapter, these ratios are explained in some detail.

Don't fret. You don't need more details of your specific retirement, not yet—that's for later in mid-career when your life has been shaped by working 15 to 20 years. Only then do you know your circumstance enough to plan for a specific retirement. Will you be married by then? Will you have kids that you need to send to college? What will your salary as well as your spouse's be at that time? Will you have a pension and/or a 401(k) plan? Will your spouse have a pension and/or a 401(k) plan? These elements will shape your particular retirement. Of course, you're free to jump ahead to Chapter 6 and see what mid-career planning is all about.

February Financial Week

How to best follow your progress toward retirement? Take one weekend a year to review where you stand financially. I suggest a weekend in February. By this time, you will have just received your end-of-year investment statements, and you'll need to get your tax information together before April 15 anyway. It's a perfect time to comprehensively check on your investments and other financial parts of your life. It's time to take stock of the previous year and set strategies for the upcoming one.

February Financial Week

Calculate your equity return for the past year.

Compare against investment benchmarks.

Rebalance your portfolio.

Set targets for savings.

Cull your records.

Your portfolio may have several investments, mutual funds, individual stocks, balance funds (which are usually about 60 percent stocks), bond funds, and so forth. Add up all the equity pieces at the beginning of the year and at the end of the year. How much did they increase or decrease, and how did that figure compare to the appropriate benchmark, or index? The most common benchmark for most stock portfolios is the S&P 500, which is discussed in the next chapter along with other indexes. So, in general, you compare the performance of your portfolio to the performance of the S&P 500.

Now you decide whether you want to rehire yourself as a money manager. If you've done well against the averages, then great. However, if your individual stock portfolio hasn't kept up, then you may wish to move to mutual funds where someone works full time managing the stocks. If your mutual fund portfolio hasn't done well, it may be time to switch to others.

You may also want to develop a "theory" of the upcoming year. It can be a guide to anticipate what could be. Do you think tech stocks or international stocks will do well? What are the trends in interest rates? Is the economy strengthening or softening? It allows you to have a general expectation of the economy and market as the year unfolds. Your theory may be right or wrong, but at least it gives you a context for making investment decisions.

You also may need to rebalance your portfolio. Your allocation may have gotten higher or lower, depending on the strength of the stock market. You may have set a target of 65 percent stocks, but perhaps the percentage has crept up to 75 percent. Over the next several months then, plan to scale back to your desired allocation.

It's also time to set any targets for savings. Should you increase your 401(k) percentage? What major expenses, if any, are you anticipating, such as redoing your kitchen or taking an extended vacation? Do you have debt that needs to be whittled down? Here, it is better to set realistic goals, like a reduction in debt of $2,000 by year end, instead of paying off all of the $20,000 debt.

What records to keep? I've had clients who—not knowing what to throw out—bring in a foot-high stack of brokerage and mutual fund statements of the past 10 years—they leave with a half-inch folder. Each year, keep the end-of-year statement and toss the monthly statements once you've completed your taxes. Do keep a looseleaf folder or desk file folder of current statements.

The Power of Saving Early and Often

How do people become financially comfortable? Slowly, one year at a time. Using a 15-year period, you can calculate the amount of money you would accumulate, depending on how consistently you saved. What if you contributed the new 2002 amount of $3,000 to an IRA for the first five years but then stopped? Table 2.1 shows you'd have $38,000 after 15 years if your money earned 8 percent. What if you waited 10 years to begin to make your first contribution? You'd only have $17,600, less than one half. Even though you would have saved five years in each case, having started early allows for the magic of compounding. But what if you contributed all 15 years? You'd have $81,450, or more than twice as much as saving just for the first five years (see Table 2.1). The moral of the story? Save as soon as you start working and continue each year thereafter.

What If Your Contributions or Investments Were 1 Percent More?

Let's go back to our basic 10-12-15 percent guideline. The 10 percent was for a person who just started a career. Let's say that person was age 25, earned $25,000, and started to save 10 percent of his salary, or in this case $2,500 the first year ($25,000 times 0.1 equals $2,500). However, if that person saved 1 percent more, 11 percent, over 40 years, that person's investments would have increased by $100,000, as shown in Table 2.2. A 1 percent increase in the investment return would have increased investments by $300,000. Thus, investment returns can be more significant than increases in contributions, but we only can control contributions, not the uncertainty of the market.

What if both were increased? A 1 percent increase in contributions and 1 percent increase in investment return would give a person $400,000 more in

TABLE 2.1 Saving Often and Early

YEAR	CONTRIBUTIONS		
2002	$ 3,000	$ 0	$ 3,000
2003	3,000	0	3,000
2004	3,000	0	3,000
2005	3,000	0	3,000
2006	3,000	0	3,000
2007	0	0	3,000
2008	0	0	3,000
2009	0	0	3,000
2010	0	0	3,000
2011	0	0	3,000
2012	0	3,000	3,000
2013	0	3,000	3,000
2014	0	3,000	3,000
2015	0	3,000	3,000
2016	0	3,000	3,000
Balance	$38,000	$17,600	$81,450
Return	8%	8%	8%
Contributions	$15,000	$15,000	$45,000
Earnings	$23,000	$ 2,600	$36,450

TABLE 2.2 How Much More Will You Have?

Starting at Age 25 (Earning $25,000)
Saving and Investing for 40 Years

INCREASING YOUR INVESTMENT RETURNS	INCREASING YOUR CONTRIBUTIONS			
	0%	1%	2%	3%
0%	—	$ 100,000	$ 200,000	$ 300,000
1%	$300,000	400,000	500,000	600,000
2%	600,000	700,000	800,000	900,000
3%	900,000	1,000,000	1,100,000	1,200,000

40 years. A 2 percent increase in both will provide a whopping $800,000 more. If a person contributed 10 percent as suggested at the beginning of this chapter, after 40 years that person could have a total of $1.8 million with the 2 percent addition. It almost doubles the result. Each percentage point becomes significant because it's carried out over so many years. You can also surmise, correctly, that a 1 percent or 2 percent decrease will cut short your investments by the same amounts.

As another example using this table, let's say you are age 25 earning $25,000, but instead of contributing 10 percent to your savings and investments you contribute 13 percent. Table 2.2 shows that given these assumptions, you would have $300,000 by the time you retire.

Of course, you might not be earning $25,000 at age 25. Perhaps your earnings are $21,000 or $32,000. Can you use this table? Although it is only accurate for this $25,000 example, the table can give you the general idea of the impact of increasing (or decreasing) contributions and investment returns by percentage points.

Life Happens along the Way

Sure, you may get pensions or stock options along the way, along with Social Security. But at the start of your career, you can only do general planning. Once you get along in your career, then you can factor in financial goodies that may come your way.

You are probably single when you first use the 10-12-15 percent rule. But then, you might get married and your spouse may also be saving at this clip. One of you may stay home for a few years to raise children, forgoing savings by one spouse. Or, you might get divorced, and money must be reapportioned. Inheritances may make retirement more attainable.

Many events may alter a linear scenario toward retirement. They are called life. But you have to start somewhere, and you can't get anywhere if you don't start to save. Eight percent investment earnings times zero savings is still zero.

Honors Section

Here are several technical aspects of retirement planning that you may want to review. They will add a dimension to your planning by providing an in-depth look at how retirement calculations are done. They include:

- Present and future value of money
- Replacement ratios
- Investment/inflation differential
- Monte Carlo technique
- Mathematical caveat

A Basic Tool: Present and Future Value

Financial planners have special tools for projecting the value of money into the future, or vice versa, for relating a future value back into today's value.

There are three sets of present and future calculations: *single amounts* of money, like CDs in a bank, *annual contributions,* with equal amounts like $3,000 (beginning in 2002) added to an IRA each year, or *increasing contributions,* like a 401(k) plan where you automatically increase your yearly contributions as your salary increases.

> **DEFINITIONS**
>
> **FUTURE VALUE**
> The value of something in the future.
>
> **PRESENT VALUE**
> How much something in the future is valued today.

Here's an example of a *single amount.* Let's say you had $10,000 in a CD, or any investment to which you were not adding money. In other words, it would just grow by itself. How much would it be worth in 5, 10, or 15 years? Table 2.3 shows factors to multiply.

If $10,000 earned 4 percent a year, it would be worth $14,800 in 10 years ($10,000 times the factor of 1.48 [4 percent for 10 years] equals $14,800). If it earned 8 percent, it would be worth $21,600 in 10 years. Table 2.3 is extracted from the longer *Table 6.1* in Chapter 6. Just multiply the amount you start with by the factor in the table.

Here's an example of *annual contributions.* This is where you add an equal amount to an investment each year, like an IRA. Let's say you want to calculate

TABLE 2.3 Future Value—Single Sums

	INVESTMENT RETURNS		
	4%	8%	12%
5 years	1.22	1.47	1.76
10 years	1.48	2.16	3.11
15 years	1.80	3.17	5.47

TABLE 2.4 Future Value—Annual Contributions

	INVESTMENT RETURNS		
	4%	8%	12%
5 years	5.52	6.10	6.73
10 years	12.25	15.07	18.60
15 years	20.40	28.23	39.51

how much your IRA would be worth after 5, 10, or 15 years, adding $3,000 to the IRA each year. Table 2.4 shows the factors for this calculation.

If you contributed the new limit of $3,000 to an IRA each year and it earned 8 percent, it would be worth $45,210 in 10 years. The table assumes that the contribution would be made throughout the year, or at mid-year.

Here's an example of *increasing contributions* where you add an increasing amount of money to an investment, like your 401(k). Although it is a more complicated calculation, it can be put in similar table form.

Let's say you contributed 10 percent of your $25,000 salary (with no employer match) and your investment averaged 8 percent per year. Your first-year contribution would be $2,500, and it would increase 3 percent thereafter, assuming that your salary would increase by 3 percent, which would automatically increase your contributions. After 10 years, your plan would be worth $42,375 ($2,500 times 16.95 equals $42,375). Table 2.5 is extracted from the longer *Table 6.2* in Chapter 6.

To combine an existing balance with additional contributions, add the single sum result with the increasing contribution result. If you have $10,000 in your 401(k) plan and currently contribute $3,250 a year, your investments are estimated to grow at 8 percent, and you are anticipating 3 percent salary increases, in 10 years you'll have $76,687 ($21,600 from the existing $10,000 plus $55,087 from the new contributions).

TABLE 2.5 Future Value—Increasing Contributions

	INVESTMENT RETURNS		
	4%	8%	12%
5 years	5.85 (3%)	6.45 (3%)	7.10 (3%)
10 years	13.91 (3%)	16.95 (3%)	20.75 (3%)

What Are Replacement Ratios?

Many retirement articles state that you need 75 percent, or a similar percentage, of your income to retire comfortably. That's a replacement ratio. Actually the ratios range from 75 percent down to 60 percent depending on your salary and your eligibility for Social Security. We used the 65 percent in determining the 10-12-15 percent savings rate because it's a reasonable average.

For example, if you earned $50,000 (gross salary) just before you retired at age 65, on average you'd need only 65 percent of that salary to keep your lifestyle intact. In this case, if you received $32,500 in retirement income (gross income) in benefits, Social Security, and investments, you'd have, on average, the same net income, $30,650, to maintain your lifestyle in retirement that you had while working. Table 2.6 shows this.

Why don't you need 100 percent of what you earned before retirement? Because in retirement your taxes are lower, in many cases significantly lower, you don't need to save for retirement anymore, and on average your expenses are somewhat less.

Can You Use the Investment/Inflation Differential?

The answer is no, but it requires an explanation. Some people try to shortcut the normal projection of one's retirement expenses and investments, year by year. They try to use the difference between projected investment earnings and projected inflation as an intuitive shortcut. Say, if investments can grow at 8 percent and inflation is estimated at 3 percent, why not just use 5 percent—the differential—to project the total of your investments? It doesn't work because your expenses and investments are different amounts.

TABLE 2.6 Replacement Ratios

Gross salary	$25,000	$50,000	$100,000
Net salary	17,500	30,650	52,200
Replacement ratio	72%	65%	63%
Retirement income	$ 7,650	$18,500	$ 46,000
Social Security	10,350	14,000	17,000
Total retirement income	18,000	32,500	63,000
Net retirement income	17,500	30,650	52,200

An example should make this clear. Let's say that your yearly retirement expenses are $75,000 and your investments are $1 million. If the investments increased 8 percent per year, or in this case $80,000, the increase in investments alone would be more than enough to cover expenses. You have to separately project your expenses and investments and determine how much of the investments are needed for your expenses; then you will see what your investments total at the end of the year.

In the improbable circumstance that your expenses and investments were equal (i.e., your retirement expenses were $75,000 and your total of investments also $75,000), then, you could use the differential because the amounts would be the same. Both would grow at their respective percentages, and the differential would be meaningful.

But, we all have different amounts, thus differential shortcuts aren't allowed.

How Can Monte Carlo Help?

No, we're not talking about going to a casino in that Mediterranean mecca and winning at roulette. We're talking about using an advanced mathematical technique commonly employed by engineers and statisticians to determine a range of probable outcomes.

The technique is beginning to be used by some financial planners in retirement projections and involves calculating a range of probable investment returns, not just, say, an average 8 percent. By running the numbers for many different returns, you can see how your retirement finances would fare if the market did worse or better. In the 1970s, the stock market only averaged 5.9 percent per year, whereas in the 1980s and 1990s, it averaged about 18 percent.

The leading proponent of this approach is Lynn Hopewell, Chairman of The Monitor Group, Inc., of Fairfax, Virginia. "The Monte Carlo technique is probably the best way to deal with this uncertainty," Lynn states, "but the practical problem is how to present this information to a client." A common output shows complicated charts with multiple probabilities.

The output might show that you will have a 50 percent chance of reaching your target of $1 million at retirement; but then it might show that you could have a 30 percent chance of having a low of $750,000 or a high of $1.25 million. Since we usually don't deal with probabilities, we may feel uneasy knowing how to interpret these probabilities. It's the same difficulty as deciding whether to take an umbrella to work if the weather report says there is a

60 percent probability of rain. A suggestion: Go with probabilities of 68 percent or higher, or two-thirds chance.

Although the investment return is one of the critical variables for retirement planning, other variables could also affect the outcomes, such as the amount of salary before retirement, increases in inflation, and yearly expenses. If you earned more money, you could add more money to your investments. If inflation increased more than expected, you wouldn't be able to add as much to your investments. If you had an unplanned expense, or an unexpected inheritance, or you decided to upgrade your lifestyle, more or less would be available for investments. Any or all of these variables could affect how much money you would have for retirement.

The advantage of the Monte Carlo technique, however, is that you generally become acutely aware that you may not meet your investment goals, given the uncertainty of the stock market.

Mathematical Caveat

When using mathematical techniques, the results are so precisely concluded that they appear to be cast in stone, when the results will only have been meticulously manipulated guesses.

But you don't need to perform fancy calculations early in your career. You only need to focus on saving 10-12-15 percent of your salary.

CHAPTER 3

Investing Is Three Parts Technical, Two Parts Psychological, One Part Faith

O ver the past year, you probably lost a great deal of faith in the stock market. With the market averaging 30 percent in each of the five years from 1995 through 1999, it didn't prepare you for the downturn. What were you to believe? It seemed that investments always went up. Although Alan Greenspan said it was irrational exuberance, you didn't want to hear that.

The problem is that those averages give little consolation to the person who gambled with a high percentage of tech stocks and now must work several extra years. It gives little consolation to the family that was 100 percent in the market to send their kids to college, and now must dip into their 401(k) and IRA funds to pay that expense, delaying their plans for retirement. Retirement delayed is retirement denied.

In one of the most dramatic cases I have come across, a couple went from $1.9 million in 2000 to $600,000 in 2001. Their retirement plan took a disastrous U-turn. They wanted to maximize their return and loaded up their portfolio with 100 percent tech stocks. They were honest, however; it was their fault. They had even asked their broker for advice and were told to cut back and buy some bonds. But they couldn't bear to cut back until they reached their goal of $2 million, so close at hand.

Let's be clear about one thing: Over the long haul, the market does well. Since 1926, the market has averaged 12 percent, while other investments have placed a distant second. In the short run, it can either be very good, very bad, or just average.

But statistics are of little use for what to do now. In brief, here are three suggestions depending on your situation:

1. If you've lost a lot of money, 50 percent to 60 percent or more, redirect your portfolio for the long term. Set your allocation to a more reasonable 60 percent to 65 percent in a diversified portfolio of stocks. You were undoubtedly too aggressive. Dwelling on the past has little productive value.

2. If you're down 20 percent to 30 percent, you're probably investing correctly. That's not to say that you feel particularly good about the situation. You may want to cut back 10 percent, or more on stocks, or if you have 10 years or more to retirement, stay where you are.

3. If you're new to investments, now is the time to slowly get into the stock market. The best news for you is the down market. On the surface, it can seem to be the worst of times, and it is for those heavily in the market. But, for you, new to investing, it couldn't be a better time.

Testing Your Investment IQ

Here are five basic questions:

1. What is asset allocation?
    a. Determining what percentage of small cap stocks should be in your portfolio.
    b. Finding the mix of stocks and bonds that is appropriate for you.
    c. Deciding how many asset classes you can add to your portfolio.
2. What is risk tolerance?
    a. The percentage of your portfolio that should be in international stocks.
    b. One's tolerance for change.
    c. The level of market volatility you can reasonably deal with.
3. What is the S&P 500?
    a. The largest 500 companies by sales.
    b. The largest 500 companies by earnings.
    c. The largest 500 companies by market capitalization.

4. What is market capitalization?
   a. The price of one share of company stock multiplied by the number of shares outstanding.
   b. The number of shares traded in any one day.
   c. The number of new shares a company sells during the year.
5. What is a P/E ratio?
   a. The price of a stock divided by its future earnings.
   b. The price of a stock divided by its current earnings per share.
   c. The productivity of a company divided by its use of energy.

(Answers: 1-b, 2-c, 3-c, 4-a, 5-b)

Here are five advanced questions for extra credit:

1. What is meant by growth and value stocks?
   a. Something we all want: growth of our investments and ability to buy them at a low price.
   b. Growth stocks have a higher P/E ratio than value stocks. Value stocks have less.
   c. Value stocks are in general more valuable to have in your portfolio.
2. What are asset classes?
   a. Large cap, small cap, and international stocks.
   b. Market segments like banking, airlines, and utilities.
   c. Classes of stock of the same company, such as Class A and Class B stock.
3. Market timing means?
   a. Being able to pick the right time to buy stocks.
   b. Going in and out of the market at the right time.
   c. Buying low and selling high.
4. What is a staggered ladder of maturities?
   a. Stocks that offer a ladder of risk tolerance.
   b. Stocks that offer a laddered level of dividends.
   c. A bond portfolio, such as Treasury notes, that have staggered maturities, such as 2-, 5-, and 10-year maturities.
5. What is meant by the efficient market hypothesis?
   a. Brokers can buy stocks more efficiently than individuals.
   b. The market is efficient but not effective.
   c. A theory that all the relevant information is known to investors.

(Answers: 1-b, 2-a, 3-b, 4-c, 5-c)

Back to the Basics

So, if it's back to the basics, just what are those basics? They're like a well-conceived recipe that combines several ingredients:

- Three parts *technical.* Asset allocation, interest rates, and assessing how you're doing.
- Two parts *psychological.* Avoiding noise and learning to do nothing, or almost nothing, once you've set up your portfolio.
- One part *faith.* If U.S. businesses continue to do well, it should be reflected in our economy and then positively in the stock market.

Three Parts Technical

Asset Allocation and Stocks

We combine stocks and bonds because we can't take the volatility that 100 percent stocks give us. Plus, we might want a steady income, say for retirement, which bonds can give us.

Although we give up maximum gains when the market does well, by having a balance of stocks and bonds, we avoid ulcers through a more stable portfolio. We are, in general, risk averse, and a balanced portfolio gives us a measure of comfort.

It also helps with another human trait: The fallacy of the straight line. When stocks go up, as they did from 1995 through 1999, people assume it will continue on and on. On the other hand, if the market crashes, then people tend to think that the downturn will continue indefinitely. Allocation diversifies the portfolio and preserves more of its value in bad years.

Table 3.1 lists some bad years and shows how your portfolio's value would have fared if it had been all in stocks or diversified.

In other words, invest in bonds, CDs, and money market funds to stabilize your overall portfolio when the market gets rough.

DEFINITION

ASSET ALLOCATION
The percentage of stocks, or stock mutual funds, in your portfolio.

We don't have a machine to hook up to you to determine your most desirable asset allocation. You determine it by guesses, trial and error, and education. The definition of asset allocation: the percentage of stocks, or stock mutual funds, in your portfolio.

TABLE 3.1   The Worst Investment Years

	100% STOCKS 0% BONDS	80% STOCKS 20% BONDS	65% STOCKS 35% BONDS	35% STOCKS 65% BONDS
1962	−8.7%	−5.8%	−3.7%	0.5%
1966	−10.0	−7.1	−4.9	−0.5
1973	−14.7	−10.8	−7.9	−2.1
1974	−26.5	−20.0	−15.2	−5.5
1981	−5.0	−2.0	0.1	4.4
1990	−3.2	−0.6	1.3	5.2
2000	−9.1	−4.8	−1.5	5.0

Note: Stocks are the S&P 500 and bonds are intermediate Treasury securities.

This is not a precise science. The best we can do is give a range. For example, we can say you should be 60 to 65 percent in stocks, specifically if you're a growth investor, or about 30 percent if you're a conservative investor.

Then, how do you feel about this percentage as you think about your investments? This will calibrate it upward or downward. The definition of risk tolerance: the amount of decrease you can take, or tolerate, in your overall portfolio. If you can't take more than about 5 percent, then you're a conservative investor; at 10 to 15 percent you're a growth investor.

> **▌DEFINITION▐**
>
> **RISK TOLERANCE**
> The amount of decrease you can take, or tolerate, in your overall portfolio.

Here are asset allocation guidelines given the type investor you are:

- An aggressive investor—80 percent in stocks
- A growth investor—65 percent in stocks
- A conservative investor—35 percent in stocks

Once you have selected this initial percentage, try to assess the level of risk tolerance you might have by how much you could lose in any one year. If you're an aggressive investor with 80 percent in the market, then you have to consider that you could lose 15 to 20 percent or more in a down year. A growth investor should expect to lose about 10 to 15 percent in a bad year. A conservative investor should expect to lose about 5 percent. This will help you further determine the percentage of stocks or stock mutual funds as a percentage of your portfolio.

DEFINITIONS

CAP
Short form for capitalization. The price of one share times the number of shares outstanding.

LARGE CAP
A reference to large companies, like Microsoft, General Electric, and ExxonMobil. Often $10 billion and larger.

MID-CAP
A reference to companies like Southwest Airlines that have established themselves but are not yet in the largest category. Often $1 or $2 billion up to $10 billion.

SMALL CAP
The struggling-to-be-noticed stocks. Often $500 million to $1 billion.

Once you set this allocation percentage, you need to determine in which asset class of stocks you will invest. As a starting point, my general recommendation for your equity portfolio is 80 percent U.S. large cap stocks, 10 percent U.S. small cap stocks (which would include aggressive tech stocks), and 10 percent international stocks.

If you can't decide how to implement an allocation or asset class strategy, start with a S&P 500 mutual fund for your portfolio. The S&P 500 has beaten most U.S. large cap funds over many years, so having the bulk of your money there is as good a place as any. Most brokers or mutual funds have diversified small cap funds as well as a diversified international fund to round out your portfolio.

Indexes for small cap funds are a little trickier. It seems that active managers can and do beat the Russell 2000 index. But, the better small cap funds get noticed quickly and often have their performance suffer. They lose their flexibility with an influx of considerable new money. Thus, for small cap stock funds, you have to look around and then be on the lookout for replacements.

For international funds, like small caps, you have to look around and be willing to change funds if your investments lag behind. Currency exchange rates can and do affect international returns. As an investor in international stocks, you desire a decreasing dollar because that magnifies positively any gains overseas.

An interesting strategy of buying into stocks is called *dollar cost averaging*. Instead of leaping with your entire savings into stocks, you do so gradually. Each month, or quarter, you buy the same dollar amount, say $500. That's what you do automatically in 401(k) plans. If stocks are up, you end up buying few shares. If stock prices are down, then you end up buying more.

After taking care of the stock portion of your portfolio, how should you invest the other part, bonds, money market, and so forth?

All the Indexes You Need to Know

Dow Jones Industrial Average. An index of the price of 30 major industrial stocks.

Standard & Poor's 500. The largest 500 domestic companies based on capitalization. The capitalization of the S&P 500 is about 75 percent of the stock market (New York, American, and NASDAQ). The S&P 500 comprises 400 industrials, 40 utilities, 40 financial, and 20 transportation companies.

Russell 2000. Consists of smaller capitalization stocks. It is a subset of the larger Russell 3000, which is an index of the largest publicly held companies. Companies in the Russell 2000 generally have a market value of $250 million or less. The index represents about 11 percent of the market capitalization of the Russell 3000.

EAFE. Stands for Europe, Australasia and the Far East. This Morgan Stanley index represents the major stock markets outside the United States. It comprises about 1,000 individual stocks.

Lehman Brothers Aggregate Bond Index. A bond index that combines government, corporate, and mortgage-backed securities. The index is considered a good gauge of bond income and price fluctuation.

Interest Rates and Bonds

There is a great economic story of the 1980s and 1990s that few appreciate, or even know. Since World War II up to the 1980s, we experienced average four-year business cycles, sometimes three years, sometimes five years. Like clock-work, inflation rose after a few years of boom times, and there is usually only one way to stop inflation—a recession. Thus, we were caught in a boom-inflation-recession cycle.

In the late 1970s, monetary policy was emerging as a possible way out of this negative cycle. Early in the 1980s, under Fed Chairman Paul Volcker, interest rates were controlled long enough to squeeze inflation out of the economy. As predicted, it caused a severe recession. Everyone held their breath, and it worked. We broke the back of inflation.

With inflation tamed, the economy entered into a long upward trend. It also broke the four-year business cycle. Eight years passed before the 1990 recession and 10 years before our current 2000 to 2001 slowdown (see Table 3.2).

TABLE 3.2 S&P 500 Year-by-Year: Annual Returns in the Stock Market from 1960 through 2000

YEAR	RETURN (%)	YEAR	RETURN (%)
1960	0.47	1970	4.01
1961	26.89	1971	14.31
1962	−8.73	1972	18.98
1963	22.80	1973	−14.66
1964	16.48	1974	−26.47
1965	12.45	1975	37.20
1966	−10.06	1976	23.84
1967	23.98	1977	−7.18
1968	11.06	1978	6.56
1969	−8.50	1979	18.44
Average	7.8		5.9
1980	32.42	1990	−3.17
1981	−4.91	1991	30.55
1982	21.41	1992	7.67
1983	22.51	1993	9.99
1984	6.27	1994	1.31
1985	32.16	1995	37.43
1986	18.47	1996	23.07
1987	5.23	1997	33.36
1988	16.81	1998	28.58
1989	31.49	1999	21.04
		2000	−9.11
Average	17.5		18

Source: Courtesy of The Vanguard Group.
Note: Average 1960–2000: 13.
    Average 1926–2000: 13.

So, how does this help with the nonequity portion of your portfolio? Your nonequity is in bonds, CDs, and money market funds, for which interest rates are key.

Bonds are long-term investments that pay a fixed interest. For example, a corporation may issue a 20-year bond to build a new manufacturing plant. The

The Fundamental Theorem of Bonds

Like a playground seesaw, the value of bonds goes up when interest rates go down, and vice versa, the value of bonds goes down when interest rates go up.

factory will take several years to plan, build, and to start making money. The bond finances such projects by spreading out its payback obligation.

The bond holder usually pays $1,000 per bond, which is repaid at maturity. (Some can be called early.) You buy bonds either with your broker, or mutual fund broker, or automatically if you buy a bond mutual fund. Balanced, or hybrid, mutual funds are often 40 percent in bonds.

Are individual bonds or a bond mutual fund for you? One offers control, the other flexibility. If you hold individual bonds to maturity, you have your $1,000 back. However, a mutual fund will have a fluctuating value. If you need extra money, you would need to sell a whole bond to get at the principal, whereas the mutual fund can just send you a check.

The federal government issues Treasury bills, notes, and bonds, which are considered the safest of all investments. Bills have a short maturity of 3 months or 6 months; notes range from 2 years to 10 years; bonds are 20 and 30 years. Municipalities offer bond issues to build local projects, bridges, and tunnels. They are tax free and appropriate if you're in the highest tax bracket.

Other nonequity investments are CDs and money market funds. CDs lock in interest rates typically for 6 months to 5 years. Both CDs and money market funds have stability of principal plus an interest rate. CDs provide a flat rate, whereas money market funds have an interest rate that fluctuates as interest rates go up or down. Mutual funds often have higher rates than banks.

An interesting bond strategy is a *staggered ladder of bonds.* If you had say, $50,000, you could buy five T-notes ranging from 2 years to 10. You would then have $10,000 in different maturities. In two years, the first note would mature and you would reinvest that money in a new 10-year note, the longest maturity. This simple strategy gives steady cash flow and takes all the anguish out of deciding what to do with the maturing money. Also, since you hold each issue to maturity, you don't have to worry about the fluctuating values of the notes or bonds.

A Staggered Ladder

Here is an example of $50,000 in a staggered ladder of Treasury notes:

- $10,000 in 2-year notes
- $10,000 in 4-year notes
- $10,000 in 5-year notes
- $10,000 in 7-year notes
- $10,000 in 10-year notes

You may not be able to set up the ladder all at one time. It may take a number of months until the Treasury issues the maturity you're looking for. Or, you can have a brokerage firm set up the ladder with existing notes.

Assessing How Well You're Doing

With these elements of allocation, stocks, bonds, and money market in mind, we can assess how we're doing each year. At least once a year, preferably after you get your end-of-year statements, you sit down and compare how you did versus the indexes. At the end of the year, there is usually a flurry of articles about how the market did for the year. This gives you the data to compare against your own returns. Having an annual February Financial Week as described in Chapter 2 is ideal for assessing your portfolio.

An Important Number: Duration

If a bond's duration is 5, then for every full percentage point increase in interest rates, the bond's value will fall 5 percent, and vice versa.

Generally, a long bond (or long bond fund) with a maturity of 30 years has a duration of about 10, an intermediate bond with a maturity of 7 years has a duration of about 5, and a short-term note or bond of 3 years has a duration of about 2.

Duration is a mathematically derived number. It is the weighted present value of all projected bond cash flows.

Here is where you need to compare apples to apples. You should answer this question: How much were you in the market and how did that portion compare with the appropriate market index? If you had all your stock money in diversified large cap stocks and funds, then compare it with the S&P 500 index. Segments in small cap or international should be compared against the Russell 2000 and EAFE.

Now comes the hardest part. Based on the results for the year, you need to decide whether you want to hire yourself again as a money manager, or get someone else to help you. If you've done well, congratulate yourself and set your portfolio for another year. If you're disappointed, then you need to find a better way.

If you've been in individual stocks, you may want to go with funds. If the funds you selected were out of sync with the market, you may want to go back to the basics and stay with mainstream funds like the S&P 500.

Finally, you may have to rebalance your portfolio. Given a year's worth of gains or losses, you may need to adjust your portfolio to stay at your preferred allocation.

A *weighted average* is most helpful in analyzing your investment return. It can determine what your projected average investment return should be given average or general rates of returns and given your investment mix of stocks, bonds, and money market funds (or whatever investment mix). It weights the return based on the percentage of each investment. Let's say your investment portfolio has 65 percent stocks, 25 percent intermediate bonds, and 10 percent money market funds. Further, let's say we assume that the stock market should increase 12 percent a year, intermediate bonds 6 percent, and money market funds 4 percent. Then we can determine our overall average annual investment return; in this example it is 9.7 percent, as shown here:

A Weighted Average

	RETURN (%)	PERCENTAGE	RESULT (%)
Stocks	12	0.65	7.8
Bonds	6	0.25	1.5
Money market	4	0.10	0.4
			9.7

Each projected investment return is multiplied by the percentage of the portfolio: 12 percent for stocks that are 65 percent of the portfolio would contribute 7.8 percent return to the portfolio (12 percent times 0.65 equals 7.8 percent). Likewise bonds would contribute 1.5 percent and money market 0.4 percent. Then add the final column to obtain the overall projected portfolio return of 9.7 percent (7.8 percent plus 1.5 percent plus 0.4 percent equals 9.7 percent).

Two Parts Psychological

Avoiding Noise, Temptation, and Distractions

Yes, the recipe for investing includes asset allocation, interest rates, and knowing how you've done, but the best strategies fall apart when our emotions take over.

No matter what investment strategy you focus on, you are still prisoner to two inescapable human forces that will in large part determine how successful you are with investing: Getting past the noise and learning to do almost nothing once you've set up your portfolio.

Each day there is a story on Wall Street. Noise. Stocks up or down. You think to yourself: "Damn, if only I was in, or out, of the market" or "If I only bought that particular stock." You could be a millionaire by now. What really gets to you: Your fellow workers may be doing well and you're not.

Our emotions tell us the bad news, but our intelligence needs to remind us to remain faithful to a well-placed strategy. Our emotions make us frustrated. Our intelligence allows us to pursue a reasoned long-term investing strategy. Our emotions can force us into short-term zigs and zags that lead you nowhere—adrift and without a strategy.

The biggest noise seems to be another human trait—the immediate past seems 100 percent inevitable. Whatever happened seems absolutely obvious after the fact. It can lead you to a false conclusion. That you could have predicted or anticipated what happened. It's not true. It's a mind game. Just test yourself. Do you know what will happen for the rest of the year, or next year? It's not obvious at all.

Robert Frost had to choose from only two paths of life one wintry night, as he stopped by a snowy wood. You have about six:

1. *Scared.* Stay out of equities.
2. *Uninformed.* Hit or miss, mostly miss.

3. *Steady as she goes.* The intelligent strategy.

4. *Lottery mentality.* Win big, quickly, with a scheme.

5. *Desperate.* All in stocks no matter what.

6. *Crap shoot.* Win big without a scheme.

Thus, you have only one in six chances to do the right thing.

Learning to Do Nothing

There is a study that shows women are better investors than men. Interestingly, the study concluded they are better because, and only because, they make fewer changes to their portfolios. More often than men, they do nothing.

As professionals have learned, progress requires being proactive. However, caution and patience are often the watchwords for investments. Once you've set your strategy in motion, you are often better doing nothing in investments. I often tell people not to read the paper or listen to the news once their portfolio is set up because keeping constant surveillance is like trying to watch grass grow.

Sometimes action can be counterproductive. People tend to sell stocks that are winners and keep stocks that are losers. Why? Because people don't like to lose money; no matter how much it hurts to hang onto a poorly performing stock, selling it turns paper losses into actual losses.

There is a management game called the Desert Exercise. You and a small number of co-workers are downed in the middle of the Sahara Desert. You're all safe, but what to do? The answer most managers give is to be active—head out to find help. The solution, however, is to stay put and try to signal airplanes. Experts explain that you would dehydrate in short order if you left the plane.

Sector funds or aggressive growth funds are another matter. These funds tend to be the most volatile. A sector may be the hot fund for only so long, like tech funds in 1999 and utility funds in 2000. Thus, close monitoring is necessary, and you may need to get out of them when they have spent their course.

We try to run a long-term race with short-term results. In our frenetic society, we expect to have information at our fingertips and to act on it. But knowing that stocks were down 3 percent last week doesn't do anything for us, except make us frustrated.

In the past, 90 percent of the investors were individual investors, now 90 percent are sophisticated institutions. It's very hard to compete against organizations with huge amounts of information and analysis and 100 percent dedication to the market.

Finally, there's an interesting theory, called the Harvest Theory, that could explain some of the ebb and flow of investments each year. Is there a seasonality about stocks? Just as the agrarian and hunter-and-gatherer societies saw the year as an annual growth and rebirth cycles, stocks, too, at times seem to play out this calendar year cycle.

Growth often occurs early in the year and spring. Frequently, there is a summer rally when the temperature is fine and the living is easy. In the fall, particularly October, dangers lurk—the coolness in the air can foretell a market fall. It appears to give an anthropological rationale for looking at a calendar year with respect to your investments.

Whether this theory has any validity, patterns do emerge during the year, or year to year. This action gives investors further reason to respond emotionally, when they should only do nothing.

One Part Faith

No matter at what point we are in our economy, business cycles expand and contract. But because you are a long-term investor, you still must have faith in the ability of our businesses and people to produce products and services that will be reflected in increasing stock market prices.

Why this faith? Because if you believe that our economy will remain on the cutting edge of technology or strong in basic but mundane businesses, then you have faith to continue to invest in stocks, short-term, mid-term, and long-term.

What happens if the economy and stock market goes bump in the night? If you're a long-term investor, stay the course because you have faith in our economy.

The Ideal Portfolio Recapped

Here then is the all-weather portfolio that should be your starting point if you're a growth investor (see Figures 3.1 and 3.2):

65 percent in stocks:
- 80 percent in large domestic stocks (about 50 percent of total portfolio)
- 10 percent in small cap stocks (about 8 percent of total portfolio)
- 10 percent is in international stocks (about 8 percent of total portfolio)

FIGURE 3.1 Simple allocation of investments.

35 percent in bonds and money market funds:

- 80 percent in intermediate bonds (about 26 percent of total portfolio)
- 20 percent in money market funds (about 8 percent of total portfolio)

You need to decide if you will buy individual stocks or mutual funds. If you're not sure, then opt for mutual funds, at least at first.

To decide whether you should buy no-load mutual funds or buy mutual funds through a broker or financial planner and pay commissions, answer the following question. Can you do it yourself? If yes, then opt for no-load mutual funds. If not, then turn to a financial planner or broker. A financial planner either will set up a mutual fund portfolio initially, which you then maintain or, more commonly, will set it up and continue to manage it for you.

To select which mutual funds, take a particular family of funds that you feel comfortable with after reading and exploring articles and books. Vanguard, Fidelity, T. Rowe Price, Janus, Strong, and Scudder are examples of families. Try to use the family that can provide the variety you need. In time, you may expand to other families as well. Most families have funds in every category.

There you have it, the ideal portfolio. If in time you feel your situation requires adjustment, then adjust. You may need more income so weight may tilt toward bonds. If you need to be more conservative as you enter retirement, then adjust.

FIGURE 3.2 Complex allocation of investments.

Mutual Fund Fees Galore

Management fee. The fee for management services, picking the right stocks, and so forth. Usually a low of 0.5 percent to a high of 1.5 percent of your investments.

Load or sales commission. The upfront fee for buying the fund. Usually a low of 0.5 percent to a high of 6 percent of your initial purchase. This is usually referred to as a Class A fund.

No-load. No sales commissions or fees to buy the fund.

12b-1 fee. A special marketing fee that can be charged.

Back-end fee. A fund that charges no upfront fee, but if you withdraw any money within the first several years, there is a declining fee. This is often referred to as a Class B fund.

How You Can Implement an Investment Strategy in Your 401(k)/403(b)/457 Plan

Savings plans such as 401(k) plans originally had only 2 or 3 investment choices, but today 12 is the average. Whether you have a 401(k), 403(b), 457, or self-directed Keogh or profit-sharing plan, you have to decide what amount of money, or percentage, to invest in the various choices.

Your first decision should be what percentage is in stocks, usually stock funds, or in some cases individual stocks. You may select from index funds, like the S&P 500, or individually managed funds. Aggressive growth and international funds can give you diversification. For bond funds, you can usually choose from funds with names like fixed-income, flexible, or U.S. Treasury. Stable value or GIC (guaranteed investment contracts) funds are like CDs.

What to do with employer stock in 401(k) plans? In some cases, your company may require their contributions to remain in their stock, but some let you diversify out of it. A rule of thumb: No more than 10 percent should be in employer stock. If you have a higher percentage, your plan is at the mercy of that stock, for better or worse.

A question on which financial planners often equivocate is: Should you keep your equity portion in tax-sheltered investments (401(k)s and IRAs), or should you keep them in nonsheltered accounts to take advantage of the lower capital gains rate? My colleague, Robin Sherwood, who has an office in New Canaan, Connecticut, rightly suggests a complex answer.

Robin recommends, "Keep the same asset allocation in your sheltered and nonsheltered accounts." She explains,"When stocks go up, people tend to feel that they shouldn't sell in a nonsheltered account because there are taxes to pay, even though it's at a lower capital gains rate." She continues, "This is counter to their own instincts of using the lower tax rate."

I remember a similar tax question posed to me on television, "Paul, why would you sell now that stocks have risen so much, and there is a whopping tax to pay?" My counter: "When would you rather sell—when stocks are high, or low?"

Conclusion

Euclid would call it congruence. Investing is retirement planning, and retirement planning is investing. Perhaps this is a little overstated, because you need to save before you can invest, but investing is the key to transforming those savings into your retirement nest egg.

So, let's start saving: On to Chapter 4.

The Sanctity of Savings (aka IRAs, 401(k)s, Keoghs) and the Dangers of Debt

Tax Highlight

RETIREMENT CONTRIBUTION LIMITS

- 2002. *IRA* contribution limits are increased to $3,000 a year, and for those 50 and over an additional $500.
  Contribution limits increase to $5,000 by 2008, and additional amounts for those 50 and over increase to $1,000 starting in 2006.
- 2002. *401(k), 403(b), and 457* contribution limits are increased to $11,000 a year, and for those 50 and over an additional $1,000.
  Contribution limits gradually rising to $15,000 by 2006, and additional amount for those 50 and over gradually rising to $5,000 by 2006.
- 2002. *SIMPLE* plan contribution limits are increased to $7,000 a year, and for those 50 and over an additional $500.
  Contribution limits are increased to $10,000 by 2005, and additional amounts for those 50 and over are increased to $2,500 by 2006.

- 2002. *SEP and Profit-Sharing* plan contribution dollar limits increased to $30,000 a year.

- 2002. *Money Purchase* plan contribution dollar limit increased to $35,000 a year.

TEMPORARY RETIREMENT SAVINGS TAX CREDIT (SEE CHAPTER 4)

- Beginning in 2002, and through 2006, a tax credit is available up to $1,000 for those contributing to a regular IRA, Roth IRA, 401(k), 403(b), 457, SEP, or SIMPLE plan. If married, you must earn $50,000 or less; if head of household, you must earn $37,500 or less; and if single or married filing separately, you must earn $25,000 or less.

DEEMED IRA (SEE CHAPTER 4)

- Beginning in 2003, organizations can set up IRAs, such as a 401(k) plan, as part of their savings plan.

INCREASED ROLLOVER FLEXIBILITY (SEE CHAPTERS 4 AND 14)

- Beginning in 2002, all 401(k), 403(b), and 457 plans can be rolled over into an IRA (including after-tax amounts), or directly into each other, if the plan allows it.

- Beginning in 2002, a surviving spouse can roll over a deceased spouse's 401(k), 403(b), or 457 plan into his or her 401(k), 403(b), or 457 plan, if the plan allows it.

Many years ago the Federal Reserve did a fascinating study about personal savings. It was a microanalysis that analyzed how individuals saved and spent money. Among several other conclusions, they determined that how you spent or saved money early in your life is to a large extent how you are still dealing with your money today. What the Fed learned then is still true today.

Your spending and saving habits are formed early in your life. If you saved most of your money from baby sitting or a paper route, then many years later you are still saving money. If you spent all your money then, many years later you are still spending most if not all of your money.

So, you are either a spender or saver. And you know which one you are. If you're married, maybe only one of you is a spender, providing a good deal of excitement in your relationship. Worse, if you both are spenders, there is probably sparse savings and some credit card debt along with a home equity loan. If you both are savers, your finances are flourishing, but you may need prodding to take that vacation you've been talking about.

We know how difficult it is to alter habits like stopping smoking, losing weight, or starting an exercise program. So, too, with savings. Don't assume that you can blithely change your ways of saving, or spending. But there are ways, which we will herein provide.

What was interesting about the study is that it offered two reasons for people's failure to save more. The first was lack of discipline, but the second was inadequate financial knowledge. Well, we're here to help with both. For the second reason, we'll go through the various retirement vehicles—401(k), 403(b), 457, SEP, Keogh, and so forth—later in the chapter. But first, let's consider the discipline issue.

Discipline

Our Consuming Hearts

Why do we spend money? That's fairly easy—it makes us feel good. Psychoanalysts explain that in our hectic everyday lives, we can often feel out of control. How do we reverse that? By switching to the buying experience. It is something that gives us control.

This predilection is true for both sexes. Women especially become pampered when they shop. They are in control, they are the boss. "I would like to see it in mauve." "Would you like to see it in another style?" "Yes, we have that in leather as well." Not that men are off the hook. Men are great with their toys. The expensive ones include big-screen TVs, Corvettes, and sailboats.

The savings experience doesn't compare. Few really enjoy saving money, except perhaps Scrooge. Saving requires long-term effort; buying brings short-term satisfaction. Saving for a downpayment for a house or condo takes real discipline, and time. Saving for retirement lasts a lifetime, or so it seems.

It's been estimated that this year, in our country of over 200 million consumers, our overall savings rate is down to an astounding zero percent. Zero percent! That's, of course, an average. It's a record we should worry about. Some economists even calculate that it's a negative percent. Actually, the Fed study found that our best savers are equal to others around the world. It's our dissavers (those negative savers) who pull us down. That's what economists euphemistically call those who dip into their savings, or worse, dig deeper in debt.

And today, we seem to live in a world with a lottery mentality. It didn't help that instant millionaires were created in the Internet stock boom. We read about corporate heads and sports figures getting record payouts. Regis asks "Who wants to be a millionaire?" And, yes, lotteries taunt us with "It could be you."

You're not taken in by these rare possibilities. You're reading this because you know that the only way you'll have the money to buy the American dream is to save and invest your money. You want to buy a condo or house, save so your child can go to a good college, and above all, you want to afford retirement. That's for sure.

The Most Powerful Way to Save

It's simple and mostly painless, and it's the most powerful way to get your dollars to savings. If you are thinking, *"payroll deduction,"* you're right. This completely unsophisticated method, of having money deducted before you can get to it, is the single most effective savings technique.

If you don't work for an organization that has a 401(k), 403(b), or 457 plan, then you have to devise one yourself. See if your organization allows a payroll deduction to a bank or mutual fund. See if your bank has a plan to automatically send an amount to investments. Prepare monthly deposit envelopes for a mutual fund and pay it first, especially into an IRA. Arrange to get a tax refund and deposit it into an investment each year, including next year's IRA.

Temporary Retirement Savings Tax Credit

Congress and the President are so worried about people not saving enough for retirement that they created a tax credit in the new tax bill. From 2002 through 2006, the new tax bill will give a tax credit up to $1,000 if you save in a regular IRA, Roth IRA, 401(k), 403(b), 457, SEP, or SIMPLE plan. You can get a tax deduction for a regular IRA (if you qualify) and get a tax credit as well! To get the credit, your earnings must be $50,000 or less if married, $37,500 or less if head of household, or $25,000 or less if single or married filing separately.

Deemed IRA

To make it even easier to save for an IRA, beginning in 2003, your organization can help by setting up an IRA, such as a 401(k), as part of your savings plan. It's called a *deemed* IRA because it's set up by your organization instead of by you. It's assumed that you are more likely to open an IRA at work when all the work has been done and the money is simply deducted from your paycheck. Not all organizations provide this service for you, so you might want to prod them to do so.

Playing Tricks to Save More

Gwen once told me how she forced herself to save for her first house. She found the most inconvenient bank. It was in another town and not even open on Saturday. She knew that once she deposited her money, it was secure. She would have to take off from work to get at it, which she wouldn't do. Each month she dutifully sent in a certain amount of savings, and thus she accumulated the down payment for her house.

Another investor told me about his brother who ordered lobster everyday on vacation, much to his father's chagrin. (The cost was of no consequence to the son.) Finally the father decided to give his son an eating allowance. It was amazing how quickly lobster got switched to tuna fish sandwiches, as the son pocketed the rest of the allowance. Both father and son were happy.

A Savings Mystery Solved

In the early 1980s, I conducted retirement seminars within a week of each other in both New York City and the New Jersey suburbs. The members of the groups were the same age and their salaries were identical; in fact, they worked for the same company. Renting was still common for New York City families, however, and most city participants were proud of their low rent-controlled apartments. Co-ops did not become common until later. Typically, the city family had no car, no equity in real estate, and curiously—little personal savings.

On the other hand, the typical suburban family was struggling to pay a mortgage and real estate taxes, had several cars besides their home equity, and surprisingly—had more personal savings! It didn't make sense.

Why did the suburban family with more financial responsibilities have more money? Why did the city family with less financial burdens end up with less? After discussing and analyzing these questions with the families, I reached an novel conclusion: Financial responsibilities force financial discipline, and financial discipline results in savings. With financial responsibilities, we often avoid frittering money away.

The Dangers of Debt

If your nonmortgage debt is more than 10 percent of your gross salary, you should set about to reduce it. If it's 15 percent or greater, you have a serious debt problem and have to get control over your credit cards and home equity debt. It erodes your financial flexibility and your long-term goal of reaching retirement on time . . . not to mention sleepless nights.

Set a realistic goal and diligently work toward it. Say, you have a debt of $5,000. You probably built it up over time, so don't think you can dispense with it quickly. Determine how much you can pay down a month and then set six-month and one-year targets: If you can afford $200 a month, then you should have $1,200 paid down with no additional debt in six months and $2,400 by the end of the year. Thus, after one year, you have only about one-half of your debt left. By the end of the second year, you should be essentially debt free, and sleeping easier.

If you're underwater and you don't see a way out of your debt situation, you need to check in with a nonprofit organization that usually goes by the title of Consumer Credit Counseling Service (CCCS). Each state or city may have its own nonprofit organization, but it usually uses a title with the CCCS name. They may also be listed on the Web.

How to Break a Bad Savings Habit

So, how can you break a bad spending/savings habit? A 12-step program? Perhaps, but here's a better idea. *The solution is to have a goal in mind.* If married, a common goal gets two people working as one. It is the most important way to break a bad savings habit—having a goal that becomes more important than spending money, like buying a condo, redecorating a kitchen, saving a specific amount of money for a potential emergency, and so forth.

Savings

- *For Everyone.* IRA, Roth IRA, bank, credit union, mutual fund, brokerage account, and annuity
- *For Employees.* 401(k), 403(b), 457, pension
- *For the Self-Employed.* SEP, SIMPLE, and Keogh: profit-sharing and money purchase plan

Chapter 14 defines distribution rules and taxes on these plans.

To have money to invest, to have enough to retire, you have to put it away in the first place. Whether it's in an IRA, 401(k), 403(b), 457, or other investments, it's getting the money there that's going to make a difference. Even dramatic investment returns can't turn a small nest egg into enough.

But savings come in many forms. Your own direct savings to a bank or mutual fund; contributions to an IRA or SEP, SIMPLE, Keogh; contributions made to a 401(k), 403(b), or 457 plan; company contributions on your behalf to a pension plan. Actually building up equity in your house, condo, or co-op is also a form of saving. They all build up assets of one kind or another.

The Individual Retirement Account (IRA)

Characteristics of an IRA

Advantage. Simple to set up and maintain.

Contributions. Maximum $2,000 in 2001, $3,000 in 2002 with an additional $500 for those age 50 and over.

Eligibility. Those who earn wages or salary, self-employment earnings, or tips, and are under age 70½.

Income limits to receive full tax deduction. $33,000 if single and $53,000 if married in 2001; $34,000 if single and $54,000 if married in 2002 (cannot take full deduction if married and file separately).

Deadline. April 15 to set up and contribute.

A regular IRA is as uncomplicated as you can get. As long as you're working, under age 70½, you can contribute up to $2,000 a year (as long as you earn $2,000) in 2001, and $3,000 in 2002. (The new tax bill recognizes that if the $2,000 IRA contributions were increased for inflation, it would be about $5,000 today.) And, if you are age 50 or over, you can contribute $500 more starting in 2002. This is called a catch-up amount. The new tax law allows for this additional amount so older workers can make up ground perhaps lost in previous years.

If you are not covered by a pension or 401(k) plan at work, there are no earning limits to get the full tax deduction. You'll know positively if you're not

Maximum Annual IRA Contributions	
2002–2004	$3,000
2005–2007	4,000
2008	5,000
IRA Catch-Up Amounts	
2002–2005	$ 500
2006–2008	1,000

covered because the box labeled "pension plan" on your end-of-year W-2 form will be marked if you are covered.

If you are covered by a plan at work, Table 4.1 lists the income limits (adjusted gross income) for you to take a tax deduction for the contribution.

In other words, for 2002, if you are single and your income is under $34,000 or you are married and your joint income is under $54,000, you can take the full deduction for your IRA contribution. If for 2002, your income exceeds $44,000 and you are single, or $64,000 and you are married, then no deduction is allowed. If you're between these limits, then you can take a partial deduction. To determine a partial deduction, complete the worksheet in the instruction booklet for Form 1040. For example, if you were single and earned

TABLE 4.1   Limits for IRA Tax Deductions

	SINGLE	MARRIED
2001	$33,000–$43,000	$53,000–$ 63,000
2002	34,000– 44,000	54,000– 64,000
2003	40,000– 50,000	60,000– 70,000
2004	45,000– 55,000	65,000– 75,000
2005	50,000– 60,000	70,000– 80,000
2006	50,000– 60,000	75,000– 85,000
2007	50,000– 60,000	80,000– 100,000

the exact midpoint in the 2001 range of $33,000-$43,000, or $38,000, then only one-half of the IRA would be deductible.

DEFINITION

FORM 8606
Used for partial and nondeductible IRA contributions, IRA conversions to Roth IRA, and Roth IRA distributions.

Nonemployed spouses can also contribute and deduct $2,000 in 2001, $3,000 in 2002 (with an additional $500 in 2002). If the employed spouse is covered under a benefit plan, the nonworking spouse's deduction is phased out beginning at an adjusted gross income of $150,000 and ending at $160,000. The contribution can still be made beyond $160,000, but it's nondeductible.

Withdrawals before age 59½ are taxed as ordinary income plus 10 percent early withdrawal penalty. Exceptions to the 10 percent penalty are disability; unreimbursed medical expenses that exceed 7.5 percent of your adjusted gross income; higher education expenses; buy, build, or rebuild your first home; distributions as a beneficiary of an inherited IRA; and substantially equal annuity payments.

The exception for disability involves a strict definition, which is the same for disability under Social Security. The exception for an inherited IRA applies to any heirs or estate that receives or withdraws any money from an IRA. Although there is no 10 percent penalty for any heir, all distributions would still be ordinary income to that heir or estate.

The exception for *substantially equal payment methods* is designed in particular for those who retire early and would like to tap their IRAs without the 10 percent penalty. The IRS allows three methods, all of which are annuity-type distributions. They are intended to deplete the IRA over your lifetime, although you only have to keep the method intact for the *longer* of five years or age 59½. For example, if you started this method at age 57, it would have to continue for 5 years, or until age 62.

One method is dividing your balance in the beginning of the year by your life expectancy. (Use Table 9.1 in Chapter 9.) Another method allows for an annuity calculation using these life expectancies and any reasonable interest rate. The final method uses any reasonable life expectancy and reasonable interest rate. Chapter 14 provides a more detailed explanation and an example.

The Roth IRA

The *Roth IRA*, named for the former Senator William Roth, is a nondeductible IRA; if held five years *and* the beneficiary is over 59½, then all withdrawals are

Characteristics of the Roth IRA

Advantage. Simple to set up and maintain.

Contributions. Maximum $2,000 in 2001, $3,000 in 2002, with an additional $500 for those age 50 and over (maximum of $2,000/$3,000 between regular IRA and Roth IRA).

Eligibility. Those who earn wages or salary, self-employment earnings, or earn tips. You *can* make Roth IRA contributions after age 70½, if eligible.

Income limits to make contribution. If your modified income is less than $110,000 if single, $160,000 if married, $10,000 if married but file separately.

Deadline. April 15 to set up and contribute.

tax-free. $2,000 is allowed to be contributed from your earnings each year in 2001, $3,000 in 2002. If you are 50 and over you can also contribute an additional $500. You cannot contribute to a Roth IRA if you've already fully contributed $2,000/$3,000 to a regular IRA for the year. To be eligible, your adjusted gross income has to be under $95,000 if single, $150,000 if married. (There is actually a phaseout of $95,000 to $110,000 if single and $150,000 to $160,000 if married).

A nonworking spouse Roth IRA is allowed, just as with regular IRAs. (You can only have one or the other, or an aggregate of $2,000/$3,000.) However, if the employed spouse earned over $160,000, then no spousal Roth IRA is allowed (nor is it allowed for the employed spouse).

The Roth IRA is generally mathematically equal to a regular IRA that is fully tax deductible. In a regular IRA, you get a tax deduction (if qualified) up front, your money grows tax deferred, and withdrawals are fully taxed in retirement. If in retirement your tax bracket is lower than today, then the regular IRA is better. In the Roth IRA, contributions are after-tax, grow tax deferred, and withdrawals are generally tax free in retirement. If your tax brackets while working and in retirement are equal, then the IRAs are equal.

However, for younger people especially (but for anyone in general), the Roth IRA has a feature that can be a real plus. A little known aspect of Roths allow for the actual contributions, not earnings, to be withdrawn at any time, even a few months later, with no tax or penalty. It obviously defeats the tax-free buildup of retirement funds, but for unexpected needs, the Roth operates as a personal savings plan.

The rule is that withdrawals first come from contributions—tax-free. Then, after the entire withdrawal of your contributions, you must wait five years (from the first Roth IRA contribution) and age 59½ before the earnings can be withdrawn tax-free. If you withdraw earnings before then, they are taxed as ordinary income plus a 10 percent early withdrawal penalty (unless you fall into one of the exceptions for regular IRAs as well).

A *Roth conversion* is an option that became available when the Roth was created in 1998, and it remains today. It allows you to pay ordinary income tax on your IRA and put the proceeds into a Roth. Because you have to pay all your taxes up front, this conversion has not been popular. It causes an immediate and heavy tax burden.

You are generally better off leaving the IRA intact and then pay your taxes a little at a time in the future when you withdraw money and perhaps will be in a lower tax bracket (which happens for most retirees). Some commentators tout the conversion by primarily stressing the eventual tax-free withdrawals and downplaying the immediate and heavy taxes owed. A present value analysis (which is the appropriate analysis) shows the advantages of keeping the money in a regular IRA versus converting to a Roth.

But, let's say you have $100,000 in an IRA and want to convert it to a Roth. First, you have to meet the requirement that your modified adjusted gross income is under $100,000, single or married (you can't if you're married filing separately). If you were in the 28 percent federal tax bracket and 5 percent state bracket, you would incur a total tax of $33,000. In other words you would immediately lose one-third of your hard-earned retirement savings, or the equivalent in another investment, to pay for this conversion. That's a big hit and a general no-no. If you've converted to a Roth in the past, you are allowed a one-time unconversion back to a regular IRA.

On the other hand, there could be estate planning reasons to convert to a Roth IRA. The owner pays all the income taxes with heirs having to pay none. Also, by paying the tax, the owner has reduced his or her estate, thereby reducing the potential eventual estate tax.

The Roth IRA, however, is always better than a nondeductible IRA (where no tax deduction was allowed). In both cases, there were no deductions and they grow tax deferred. So far equal. However, withdrawals from Roths are tax-free (if they meet the requirements), but withdrawals from nondeductible IRAs are partially taxed.

Other Ways to Save

If your employer doesn't have a plan, or you wish to put additional money away for a rainy day, open an account with a mutual fund or brokerage firm. Some employers have credit unions that allow for payroll deductions.

Regular annuities can be an effective way to save, but they generally have higher fees than other investments. Also, the equity in one's home is a way to "save" money by accumulating a valuable asset.

Your employer may offer one of the following plans:

- 401(k)
- 403(b)
- 457
- Traditional Pension and Cash Balance Plan

401(k) PLANS

Characteristics of a 401(k) Plan

Advantage. Before-tax contributions.

Contributions. Maximum of $10,500 a year in 2001, $11,000 in 2002, and starting in 2002 for those 50 and over an additional $1,000. Contribution limits gradually rising to $15,000 by 2006, and additional amount for those 50 and over gradually rising to $5,000 by 2006.

Tax on withdrawals. Ordinary income tax, can roll over into IRA or other retirement plan, and can use 10-Year Averaging if eligible (see Chapter 14 for explanation).

The 401(k) plans are named after the Tax Code section that allows them. They combine the best of all retirement saving worlds: pretax contributions; tax shelter; and in most plans, company contributions. If a company matches 50 percent of your contributions, you've just gotten a 50 percent return. Combined with pretax deferrals, you're total return is about 80 percent. Last time I checked, banks and mutual funds don't do this. The employer match is often as high as 3 percent for your first 6 percent contributions.

Because it is found money, you should in almost all cases contribute to get the full company matching contribution. If you have financial emergencies or are on a very tight budget, you may temporarily find a full contribution to be unwarranted. But otherwise there should be little reason why you shouldn't contribute to get the full company match. You simply get to retirement sooner.

Although you are always vested in your money, there is usually a time period before you vest in the company's contributions, often 3 to 5 years. Also, most 401(k) plans offer a loan provision. You can take out a loan, at current loan rates, up to 50 percent of your vested balance, to a maximum of $50,000. You pay yourself back, because your loan payments go into your own account. During the stock market meltdown, the loan portions of plans were not affected negatively. But when the market does well, you lose money when you take a loan.

Although only a small percentage of people take out loans, those who do usually overwork them. Remember that when you leave the company, you have to pay back the loan or have it counted as a withdrawal—which means that it is taxed as ordinary income and hit with a 10 percent penalty if withdrawn before age 55.

If you're a high earner and not getting the full company match, check to see if you can reduce your contribution percentage thereby getting all the match. Sometimes you can overshoot your contributions and miss the match.

You usually can't take any withdrawals while working for your company, except for a hardship withdrawal, if allowed in your plan. However, when you leave your firm, you can roll over the money or take some out. Chapter 5 reviews these options as well as the tax rules.

403(b) PLAN

Characteristics of the 403(b) Plan

Advantage. Before-tax contributions.

Contributions. Maximum of $10,500 a year in 2001, $11,000 in 2002, and starting in 2002 for those 50 and over an additional $1,000. Contribution limits gradually rising to $15,000 by 2006, and additional amount for those 50 and over gradually rising to $5,000 by 2006.

Tax on withdrawals. Ordinary income tax and can roll over lump sum into an IRA or other retirement plan.

Known formally as 403(b) plans (named after the Tax Code section that allows them), they can be called a tax-deferred annuity (TDA), or tax-sheltered annuity (TSA), or a specific plan for colleges called TIAA-CREF. They are for non-profit, medical, and other tax-exempt organizations. They operate like 401(k)s in that contributions are pretax, the most effective kind. However, most organizations do not contribute to the plan; you alone fund it. The maximum contribution for 2001 is $10,500, the same as for 401(k)s; for 2002 it is $11,000, with an additional $1,000 for those 50 and over.

A distinguishing feature of a 403(b) plan is that your employer selects several insurance companies to come in and present their investment options to you and the rest of the staff. Once you've selected the insurance firm and the investments, then your employer deducts the amount of contributions from your salary.

When you leave the organization, you are often allowed to take a lump sum, which can then be rolled over into an IRA or other 403(b) plan or other retirement plan. Since these plans are not technically classified as qualified benefit plans, you cannot use 10-year averaging on the lump sums (see Chapter 14 for explanation of tax).

Your total holdings at TIAA-CREF can be quite complicated if you have moved from one college to another. Each organization has a separate plan with TIAA-CREF, even though it's invested in the same funds. When you get close to retirement, call TIAA-CREF with your individual contract numbers. They will tell you which plans allow lump sums, fully or partially, what your investment choices are, and what annuity choices are available to you.

457 PLANS

Characteristics of the 457 Plan

Advantage. Before-tax contributions.

Contributions. Maximum of $8,500 in 2001, $11,000 in 2002, rising to $15,000 in 2006. Starting in 2002 an additional $1,000 for those 50 and over, increasing to $5,000 by 2006.

Tax on withdrawals. Ordinary income tax; beginning in 2002 can roll over into an IRA or another 457 plan or other retirement plan.

If you work for a state or local government or for some tax-exempt organizations, you may be eligible for a deferred compensation plan called a 457 plan (named after the Tax Code section that allows it). Contributions are pretax because they are a reduction of your salary. The plan defers a portion of your salary to a later date.

Distributions are *not* eligible for 10-year averaging. Why? Because 457 plans are technically deferred compensation plans, not benefit plans. Distributions are simply taxable when taken.

TRADITIONAL AND CASH BALANCE PENSIONS

Characteristics of Pensions

Advantage. Employer generally makes all the contributions.

Tax on withdrawals. Ordinary income tax, but rollover and 10-Year Averaging with qualifying lump sum.

A *pension* is technically called a defined benefit plan and usually provides a specific, or defined, monthly payment on retirement, often called an annuity. The amount usually depends on how long you've worked for the organization and how much you earn. Typically, the company contributes all the money to the pension, in contrast to a 401(k) or other savings plan where you contribute most of the money and decide on how it gets invested. Although most of the plans pay out in a monthly payment, about 20 percent of traditional pensions, and all of cash balance plans, pay lump sums.

The number of people covered under pensions is waning, although you still might be covered by one or more throughout your career. If your organization has a pension, you are usually eligible for it after five years. Also, you are usually provided an annual pension estimate called *an accrued benefit,* which is the amount of your pension if you left work now and started to collect at retirement, usually age 65. Some organizations are starting to project your age 65 benefit with an estimated salary increase between now and then.

Companies usually reduce your pension if you take it early. Some reduce it only before age 60 or 62 when you're eligible for Social Security. Some companies, however, provide incentives for you to take early retirement by lessening these reductions all the way down to age 55.

The normal actuarial reduction from age 65 is about 6.7 percent per year, the same reduction used for Social Security if you take that benefit early. If the full actuarial reduction is applied, at age 55 your benefit would be reduced about 67 percent, leaving only about 33 percent (reduction of 6.7 percent times 10 years equals 67 percent). But you are collecting it early, and the reduction takes account of this. Some organizations that want to encourage early retirement may reduce your benefit by a smaller percentage, say 5 percent per year, and some even forgo any reductions between 65 and 62 or 60.

Age 55 is a common cutoff for collecting your pension. If you want to retire before then, you generally are not entitled to an immediate benefit, and in fact may have to wait until 65 for any pension.

Some companies take a different tack and may require a total of "points," 75 or 80, before you are entitled to retire. Age plus years of service equal your total points. If you need 80 points and you are 58 with 20 years of service, you would need to wait one more year (59 plus 21 equals 80).

Another most important aspect of retiring early, besides the reduction in your pension and age of retirement, is entitlement to a retiree medical plan for the rest of your life. This is a prized benefit to be sure, if offered. Each company that offers a retiree medical plan defines its rules differently. Some will require a specific age or years of service, regardless of receiving a pension. Others will define it as meeting their age 55 early retirement definition. Thus, leaving before 55 is usually a serious retirement matter.

For *members of unions,* your pension may be what is called a *flat benefit plan.* After a specified number of years, you are entitled to a pension usually equal to a flat dollar amount times your years of service. A plan may require 20 years of service, but once there you can retire anytime with a pension equal to, say, $20 a month times years of service. In this case, if you had 30 years of service, your pension would be $600 a month ($20 times 30 years) or $7,200 a year.

A *cash balance plan* is a cross between a pension plan and a profit-sharing plan. The company still contributes most, if not all the money, but you can see what "cash balance" is in your account each year. The company, however, doesn't promise a specific benefit, like a true pension, only what your account balance will provide at retirement. The great thing about cash balance plans is you get to take your pension with you. It's portable. You can roll it over into an IRA when you leave.

Above all, when leaving a company, get in writing what pension and other benefits you're entitled to at specific ages. Plans usually allow for a single sum payout if the total value of your benefit is less than $5,000. It saves on administration costs to get rid of it. Also, know the names to contact in Benefits or Human Resources for future questions. I recommend that you recontact these people every three years or so. They are the lifeline to your retirement benefits, and if there are new contacts, you'll want their names.

Plans for the Self-Employed

If you're the boss, then you can set up a variety of plans, from the simple to the very complex. If you're in the beginning stages of your business, then the Simplified Employee Pension (SEP) and profit-sharing are usually your ticket. You only need to contribute if there are profits. Only go to the other plans when your profits become steady.

THE SIMPLIFIED EMPLOYEE PENSION (SEP)

Characteristics of the SEP

Advantage. Simple to set up and maintain.

Contributions. Not required, maximum to 15 percent of compensation or $25,500 for 2001, $30,000 in 2002.

Deadline to set up plan. April 15 or your company's tax-filing deadline.

The SEP or SEP-IRA is the easiest plan to set up, almost as easy as an IRA itself. It can be used even if the owner is the only employee. The employer must make specific contributions to an individual's SEP account.

You can contribute a maximum of 15 percent of your net salary up to $25,500 in 2001, $30,000 in 2002. The 15 percent is figured on the "net" of your income. Contributions to employees, however, are figured on their gross salaries.

Figuring the exact contribution is a little circular. Say an owner is earning $50,000 salary—the maximum that can be contributed is $6,520 (which is only 13.04 percent of $50,000). Subtracting this contribution, $6,520, from the gross salary nets $43,480; $6,520 of this net, $43,480, is 15 percent. Thus, although it's advertised as a contribution of 15 percent, that's on the net, not the gross. Therefore, to calculate the contributions directly, simply take 13.04 percent of gross salary.

You can contribute to a regular IRA as well. Thus, in this example you can contribute a total of $8,520, $6,520 plus $2,000, to an IRA. If you are married filing jointly, the IRA would be fully deductible in this example, because the salary is under $53,000 for 2001. The total in 2002 would be $9,520, with a $3,000 contribution to an IRA.

If you have employees, you must contribute an equal percentage to them, although you can have certain restrictions (e.g., they have to be employed one year and be as least 21). Contributions immediately vest for you and your employees. You have the flexibility not to contribute each year, depending on your profits. One year you can contribute 4 percent, the next year zero, the following year 7 percent, and so forth.

You can set up the plan whenever you pay your taxes, as late as April 15. Withdrawal rules are the same as a regular IRA. No loans are permitted from the SEP. It is ideal for the person in business who wants to contribute more than solely to an IRA. It's popular especially with independent contractors, consultants, and freelancers.

SAVINGS INCENTIVE MATCH PLAN FOR EMPLOYEES (SIMPLE)

Characteristics of the SIMPLE

Advantage. Relatively simple to set up and maintain.

Contributions. Required minimum and maximums. Maximum is $6,500 for 2001, $7,000 in 2002, increasing to $10,000 in 2005. Additional $500 starting in 2002 for those 50 and over.

Deadline to set up plan. Generally before October 1.

If you have a business with less than 100 employees, a SIMPLE is actually easy to set up. Because it's a tad more complex than the SEP, it has not been particularly popular. Technically it is a form of an IRA, and in fact you may see it called a SIMPLE-IRA. In a SIMPLE plan, employees make most of the contributions; however, the owner must match dollar-for-dollar up to 3 percent of the employee's contributions. The maximum employee contribution cannot exceed $6,500 per year in 2001, $7,000 in 2002. In 2002, an additional $500 will be allowed for those 50 and over.

Withdrawal rules are the same as a regular IRA after two years. Like the SEP, no loans are permitted. It's ideal for the small business owner who wants to reward employees with a 401(k)-type plan without the complications of an actual 401(k) plan. You can also contribute to an IRA if you have a SIMPLE.

KEOGH PLANS

Characteristics of Keogh Plans

Profit-sharing. **The easiest and most flexible.**

Money purchase. **A fixed contribution level is determined to provide a desired benefit.**

Defined benefit. **Allows the highest contributions but is the most complex.**

Keogh plans (named after Eugene Keogh, the representative who authored the legislation in 1962) are sometimes called H.R. 10 plans (for the legislation number that gave birth to it). It's a favorite of the self-employed who have gained a certain stability of profits. They range from simple profit-sharing to the most complex, defined benefit.

Profit-sharing plans are the most flexible of all Keogh plans. The profit-sharing Keogh is essentially the same as the SEP. Unlike the other Keogh options, the profit-sharing has the most flexibility as to the contributions. Here you don't have to make yearly contributions if profits aren't there. Once the others are set up contributions are mandated.

In 2001, you can contribute up to 15 percent of your net, or a limit of $25,500, whichever is less; and in 2002 the dollar limit has been raised to $30,000.

Money purchase plans allow for contributions that try to result in an appropriate retirement benefit or target. The money purchase plan tries to calibrate the contributions to a set retirement amount. A variation of the money purchase plan is even called a *targeted benefit plan.*

Importantly, the amount of contributions permitted are usually greater than those provided by a SEP or profit-sharing plan and thus can be more valuable, especially if the company has stable or growing profits. Since the contributions are mandatory once set up, these plans are not to be started casually. In fact, a company may start out with a profit-sharing plan and migrate to a money purchase plan once it has reached stability. Also, it's common for a company to have both a money purchase plan, for a portion as guaranteed contributions, and a profit-sharing plan, for the rest of the contributions, which can be dependent on profits. That way, not all the pension contributions would be necessary in lean years.

In 2001, the contributions can be up to 25 percent on a net income of $170,000, or up to a maximum of $30,000 per year, which ever is less; however in 2002 the dollar contributions can be up to $35,000.

Defined benefit plans are complex but allow the owner of a business to increase contributions significantly especially if over age 40. This can be particularly valuable for an owner who starts the plan late in life and can make significant contributions.

These plans are complex to set up and require an actuary to calculate the contribution amounts yearly. The actuary also calculates when your contributions top out and how the plan can be terminated when you retire.

The Bottom Line

Two last thoughts: Don't fall into the planning paralysis trap, and do set objectives. Why might your planning be paralyzed? Because there are so many investment choices, some people don't save until they find the perfect place to put their money. "There are so many mutual funds, I don't know where to start" is a common plaint. My suggestion: Keep it simple at the start with a money market fund. Once you figure out a better place, then invest accordingly. At least you've started saving money.

Many don't save because they don't set objectives—the most successful way to overcome the lack of savings discipline. Wanting to buy a house or a new car focuses the mind and gives motivation to save a specific amount of money for a specific purpose. And retirement, now that's a goal worth saving for.

CHAPTER 5

Your Financial Engine: Your Career

Today you're the head of a corporation called You. You're chief operating officer, chief financial officer, and head of marketing. In the past, organizations took care of you, saw to it that your career was on track and helped you if help was needed. When was the last time you noticed this attitude?

Does it sound like an exaggeration to say that one of the most important financial and retirement activities you can do is to *get* and *keep* your career together? Believe it. Your job, your career, and your profession are your financial engine. It provides the financial resources to make the rent or mortgage payments and provides you with the savings for retirement. It can even help in retirement if you need to return to some work to add to your income.

What Is a Career?

Although careers may be central to our financial well-being, they have a life of their own. First, we have to select a field of endeavor before we have any, or little, experience with work. Later, when we grow up and decide what we really want to do, we may find ourselves in the wrong field. And finally, since we all could successfully perform many jobs, it might be difficult to decide what our "true" lifework should be.

Careers are no longer a simple series of jobs in a specific field. In the past, you entered a company as a junior accountant, were eventually promoted to accountant, and perhaps reached senior accountant before you were 40. Then, if you worked very hard, you would be anointed as the manager of the account-ants. A career ladder.

Today, after being downsized at the accountant stage, a person may end up as a marketing rep and then try human resources. Later, the person may decide to open a small resort in the Florida Keys.

Today's *career* is a series of jobs that define you as you zigzag through life. A *job* is that position you happen to find yourself in today by circumstance and opportunity. Instead of ladders to climb, we have bridges to cross.

The 85 Percent to 15 Percent Problem

I have observed that too many people feel they can have only one chosen career or profession, and they tend to waste too much time and energy trying to find it. People can remain frozen in their jobs because they don't know what job is the perfect match for their skill-sets.

Here's a hint. Only about 15 percent of workers really know what they want and therefore have identified what to them would be their perfect job. (That's a guess after spending about 10 years in human resources, much of it in recruit-ing.) The rest of us, the 85 percent, are generally intimidated by the 15 percent because we somehow feel we should know what we should be doing.

I like to tell the 85 percenters, likely you, besides myself, that we are in fact the fortunate ones, although it may not feel like it. The 15 percenters have only one career on their minds from high school through life. It may bring certainty to a very important part of their lives, but we have the advantage of being flexi-ble about what we do. We are not confined to a specific area. We are free to pur-sue whatever path we wish. In fact, we could be successful in many endeavors, as could the 15 percent if they wanted to.

The Most Important Career Advice You Can Receive

If you can't decide on a specific career or job: Pick something, pick anything, and get good at it. You may discover another career later, but in the meantime you need to pay the bills. And don't let the 15 percent single-mindedness get to you. Plunge into a job as if it was your chosen career. It's all you've got at the moment. Then, if along the way you fall into the 15 percent category, great, pur-sue that.

Career Cycle: The Mid-Career Crisis?

A crisis can occur at any point in one's career. A 30-year-old may find himself in the wrong field, or a 35-year-old may realize she is without a career after raising a child. A telltale sign is that you're in mid-career—and you want to retire in the worst way.

The most commonly identified crisis point is midlife. Why? Some can stay in the same job and are highly motivated to do that job for a whole career. Most often, however, people seem to run out of steam after about 15 to 20 years. We're excited at first as we learn a new field. It takes several years to understand our field, several years to get good at it, then several more to master and enjoy it. The challenges keep us preoccupied. But after we master it, boredom can set in. In some fields like nursing or counseling, people often become burned out and need a change.

Solution: Either find ways to rechallenge yourself within your job or find a different job in your organization where you meet new challenges. If that is impossible, you may have to leave your employer for new pastures to reach a satisfying job.

The Pink Slip and Plan X

The pink slip can lead to RDD, Retirement Deficit Disorder, but being prepared for this eventuality is the best antidote. That means having a Plan X. You should imagine your boss telling you that you are being downsized, and you have to leave the premises immediately.

As traumatic as that is, mentally walking through that possible event ahead of time can take some of the sting out of it. Then, because you're prepared, you launch into your Plan X the very next day. That plan includes having a clear idea of jobs you would be interested in, a resume ready to submit, and a Rolodex of contacts to call. It also means having prepared for practical matters: how to give a good interview and how to deal with salary issues.

Developing a Plan X

- Hold a personal career weekend once a year.
- Analyze where you are in your career.
- Set specific goals for the year.
- Update your resume.
- Prepare several resumes, for several possible jobs.
- Continue to evolve in your career.
- Maintain contacts in your field for possible moves.

A Personal Career Weekend

Take one weekend a year to review where you stand in your career. The summer could be the best time, when you're more relaxed. Or, it could be around a career event, perhaps the anniversary of your first job, or your present job. Or, it could be the weekend after the financial weekend referred to in Chapter 2. You can combine finance and careers back-to-back in a concentrated way.

For most people, however, you may need to keep career planning separate from the nitty-gritty of investments or taxes. Careers need to focus on your skills, your objectives, your work desires, your life. It's a different ball game from the details of your finances.

Don't Kid Yourself about Job Hopping

It has been fashionable to point out that younger workers will change jobs 10 to 15 times in their careers. The problem is that loyalty may come back in vogue.

So, however many times you change jobs, make every move count. Don't move because your friends are moving or for just a few more dollars. Answer these questions: What new responsibility will you have? What new education will the new job provide? What broadening experiences will it give you? What new challenges does it offer? What new employee benefits will you secure?

Financial Moves during Your Career

Changing Jobs and the Rollover IRA

The most important retirement decision you make when you change jobs is to keep your 401(k), 403(b), 457, or other plan intact. Roll it over into an IRA or your new employer's plan, or leave it with the old employer if that's the best option. It is your portable pension fund and it should be maintained to grow tax-deferred.

You could be tempted to cash out your plan when you leave, if allowed. In fact 60 percent of the people do according to the IRS. And if you do and are under age 55, you will probably lose as much as half of it to taxes and penalties.

Here's an example. When Paula, 45, left her firm, she wanted her hands on the $25,000 in her 401(k). She and her husband were earning jointly $130,000, putting them in the federal 31 percent tax bracket and their state's 5 percent bracket. She ended up with only 54 percent of it, or only $13,500 to spend. Here's how it calculated out:

Amount cashed out from 401(k)		$25,000
Federal income tax (31% bracket)	$ 7,750	
State income tax (5% bracket)	1,250	
Early withdrawal penalty (10%)	2,500	
Total taxes and penalties	$11,500	
Amount left to spend		$13,500

Paula found out the hard way that this was a hefty price to pay for remodeling her kitchen. If this money had stayed in the plan and grown for 20 years at 8 percent, she would have had just over $116,500—more than four and a half times the $25,000.

You can generally leave the money in the plan if you have over $5,000 in the account, but you'll have to check. This is a good idea if you like the investment choices. But, do check if the employer will limit your withdrawals in the future. If so, then roll it over into an IRA where you have maximum flexibility.

If you've made any after-tax contributions, the new law will allow, beginning in 2002, for you to roll over this amount along with your other money. Previously, no after-tax contributions could be rolled over into an IRA. This is another example of Washington's efforts to see to it that you preserve all of your retirement dollars.

If the investment choices in your old plan are limited or you really don't want to interact with your former employer, then roll your money into an IRA. If you've accumulated several plan balances from various employers, you might consider consolidating them into one IRA or your new employer's plan for ease of management.

401(k), 403(b), and 457 Options

- Leave the money in the plan.
- Roll it over into an IRA.
- Roll it into your new employer's plan, if allowed.
- Pay taxes and possible penalties if you take the money out.

When you do take your money and want to roll it over into an IRA, use the *direct rollover* method. It moves the money directly to another plan without you having access to it during the move and avoids the mandatory 20 percent federal tax withholding that you don't recoup until you file your taxes. In fact, your employer will probably emphasize this to you. As a result, almost everyone who wants to roll over money into an IRA does so by this direct method.

If you did roll it over yourself (not using the direct rollover) and didn't find the equivalent 20 percent amount that was required to be withheld and also put that in the IRA, the 20 percent amount is considered a taxable withdrawal. It's dirty pool, but a method the government uses to discourage you from taking the money. Thus, unless you want the money to spend, use the direct rollover.

Also note that if you have a loan outstanding in the plan when you leave, you are almost always required to pay it off, or it will be considered a taxable withdrawal. This is true whether you leave it in the plan or roll it over.

Up to the new tax law, there was an IRA term called a *Conduit IRA.* It allowed money from one plan to be kept separate so it could be rolled over into another company plan. However, the new tax law allows for greater flexibility. Beginning in 2002, plan money can be rolled over into IRAs, combined with other IRAs, and then rolled into a new company plan, if the plan allows for such rollovers. Even if you want to move the money into your new employer's plan, you may not be able to do so for a year, depending on the new employer's rules.

If you absolutely need some of the money, you can roll over only a portion, keeping out the amount you need. The amount not rolled over will be taxed: Your employer must withhold the mandatory 20 percent withholding tax, and if you are under *age 55,* there will be a 10 percent early withdrawal penalty tax. Note that this differs from the age 59½ rule for IRAs. The 10 percent penalty applies before 55 for benefit plans, 59½ for IRAs.

If you change jobs, check whether you'll be eligible for a *pension.* Usually you need to be at your organization for five years. When you leave a company, get in writing what pension and other benefits you're entitled to at specific ages. Also, keep a record of the names to contact in benefits or human resources for future pension questions. You should recontact these people every

> ## Confusing Age 55 and 59½ Rules
>
> - If money comes from an *IRA,* then age *59½* rules.
> - If money comes from a *benefit* plan, like a 401(k) plan or pension lump sum, then age *55* rules.
>
> *Example:* If a person was age 57, there would be no 10 percent if the money came from a 401(k), but there would be if the money came from an IRA.

three years, or so. There may be many years between when you leave your organization and when you first start to collect any benefit.

Evaluating an Employer's Benefits

Before you join an organization, make an assessment of the employee benefits. Do they have a 401(k), 403(b), 457, or similar plan? Do they have a pension plan? What does their medical plan cover? How much vacation? And, any other benefits or perks? You should perform the same assessment of your current employer; then you can compare what you have versus what's greener on the other side of the fence.

When do you *start* with their plans and when do you *vest*? For many plans, you typically don't start for a year, although some may offer to start you immediately. Vesting means when you are entitled to get a benefit. Some plans vest the employer's contributions in three or five years, possibly earlier. You are always vested in your own contributions.

What percentage *contributions* does the employer offer, if any? The most common match for a 401(k) plan is 50 percent of your 6 percent contributions: If you contribute a full 6 percent of your salary, you get their full 50 percent match. It's a fantastic deal and you shouldn't pass it up. You get a total of 9 percent contributed to your account as long as you stay the required vesting time. There is no standard schedule, so you'll have to review the benefit booklets or materials.

Age 55 is usually a magic year for traditional pensions. After that, your pension can be significantly higher. So, if you're thinking of leaving your employer around 55, check to see whether it's worth while to stay a little longer. This is additionally true if you would have lifetime medical coverage if you stayed long enough, again usually at age 55 with a certain number of years of service.

Managing Your Stock Options

Companies are offering stock options to more and more people in the organization. No longer are they available only to the very few at the top. It's an area where dot-coms have left their mark—they frequently gave options to all employees.

There are two types of stock options: NQSO (nonqualified stock option, referred to simply as "nonqualified") and ISO (incentive stock option, pronounced EYE-so). The nonqualified can be popular with companies because they get a tax deduction when employees exercise them. Employees also like nonqualified because they usually exercise and sell at the same time—when the stock price is just right—a simple capturing of a windfall. Also, ISOs can cause AMT (alternative minimum taxes) problems for employees who hold the stock after exercising them.

If you've never dealt with options, here's how they work. Stock options are typically offered to you at whatever the market price is on that day, let's say 300 shares at $25. Thus, the "option" allows you to buy that stock at $25 anytime in the future, usually as long as 10 years, no matter the price at that time. You usually can't exercise all the options immediately, often you vest in them over three years, one-third after one year, one-third after the second year, and so forth.

In our example, that would make 100 shares available to you each year. You then would wait and hope for it to rise in price. If it did, then you might

AMT (Alternative Minimum Tax)

This tax was originally designed to make sure that persons with high incomes would pay their share of taxes. Many of these taxpayers were hiring accountants who used various techniques to get around the tax laws. The AMT is designed to mitigate the effects of these planning techniques and force wealthy taxpayers to pay taxes. In recent years, however, more middle-income earners have been forced to pay this tax, resulting in efforts by many in Congress to provide relief, if not eliminate it all together. The new tax law only provided minor relief.

"exercise" it, or buy it, at the original lower issue price, not the current higher price. You pay the company the original price, $25, and you've bought something that is worth more on that day, say, $40.

Finally, you decide to sell the stock at some point. To facilitate selling, most companies have engaged an outside brokerage firm to assist in this process. Actually, most employees exercise and sell options on the same day. Employees would rather lock in a certain known value, as opposed to exercising an option and have it go down in value before they sell it.

Since an individual stock can have greater volatility than the stock market in general, how do you manage the options? Perhaps the two best approaches to options are to first discern whether there are any price patterns to the stock and second set targets when you should sell.

For example, if your company follows a business cycle, then you might anticipate fluctuations from lows to highs during that cycle. This is not particularly easy, however, if business cycles have elongated, as they did in the 1980s and 1990s. Setting targets is also difficult but probably the best course. You also have excellent knowledge of the company's performance, so that should guide you in setting targets.

If the price of the stock is, say, $25 now, you could set a target of 30 percent greater, or about $33, when you might exercise. But because of the downturn in prices for some companies this past year, you might have to wait for many years for the options to get above water again.

For nonqualified options, ordinary income tax is due on the appreciation portion when you sell the options. If an option exercise price was $25 (what you bought it for) and if the stock was $40 when you sold it, you owe tax on the gain, in this case $15. For ISOs, there is no immediate tax when an option is exercised, only when sold. If you waited the long-term capital gains period before you sold an ISO option, a year and a day (and held the option for two years) then the appreciated value is taxed at the capital gains rate—20 percent for most taxpayers. If you sell an ISO early, called a disqualifying disposition, it becomes a nonqualified option and ordinary income tax is due.

What about a Buyout Offer?

As an inducement to take early retirement, companies sometimes offer sweetened pensions or severance payments. A large corporation offered Matt an additional 5 years of service to boost his pension and a full year of severance payments, very lucrative in a cold-hearted business world. At age 60,

Matt was going to retire soon anyway, so as he said, "It was golden pennies from heaven."

For Cynthia, it was another matter. She was offered the same "package," as they often refer to it, but she was only 45 and would have to work for at least 10 more years anyway. She was also told that she could continue her job as a graphics designer for now, but there might be layoffs down the road. Although her job was uncertain, she needed to work. Since she couldn't locate a similar job, she decided not to take the package and to stay on, with the hope that her job would continue for a number of years.

These two examples show how two people could come to opposite conclusions about the same buyout offer. If you have to decide on such an offer, it usually depends on how close you are to retirement. It was easy for Matt because he was ready to retire. For almost everyone else, it is a difficult decision. You should consider what you would do if you took the offer. Would you need to continue to work? If so, then you might decide not to take it. However, if you think you might be job eliminated anyway, then taking the offer would provide at least some additional money or benefits.

A Final Word

As head of the corporation called You, you need to spend time not only planning your career, but managing critical events about your benefits. Two key decisions: How much do you contribute to your employer's savings plan? (hopefully at least enough to get the full employer contribution, if available); what will you do with a plan when you change jobs? (hopefully preserve it, either by leaving it intact or rolling it into an IRA or your new employer's plan).

You may have many challenges in your career and your jobs. They compose your financial engine, but how you manage your 401(k), 403(b), and 457 plans and other benefits can in large part determine when you retire and how secure that retirement will be.

CHAPTER 6

Step 2. Mid-Career— Setting Your Glide Path to Retirement

You've reached mid-career! Congratulations. You're somewhere between 40 and 55, plus or minus, and seriously focused on retirement. It's time to establish a specific glide path to your workaday world objective, the Big R. Like a plane on a glide path coming onto a runway to land, your glide path to retirement will ensure a smooth landing.

In the chaos of your everyday life, or so it seems, you are trying to juggle myriad financial concerns—having enough for never-ending bills, affording vacations, and if you have children, most likely paying, or about to be paying, for your children's college education. It's a difficult time to see your way clear to retirement.

But you relish the thought of it, want to set a target date, and work toward it. This chapter provides two straightforward worksheets (Figures 6.1 and 6.2) that can help you determine whether your numbers meet your targeted retirement. The first worksheet determines how much income you might have at retirement, the second your expenses. Then it's a matter of matching them up.

For the *income worksheet* (Figure 6.1), you'll need a targeted retirement date, age 57, 62, 65, or whatever, and the total amount of investments you have

	YOU	EXAMPLE
Retirement investments now	_____	$ 158,000
Years to retirement	_____	20
Factor from Table 6.1 example uses 8% investment return)	_____	4.66
Retirement Value A (multiply amount of investments by factor)	_____	$ 736,280
Your current annual contributions	_____	$ 8,500
Your firm's annual contributions	_____	3,400
Total	_____	11,900
Factor from Table 6.2 (example uses 20 years, 8% return, and 3% increases)	_____	59.38
Retirement Value B (multiply contribution total by factor)	_____	$ 706,622
Total Value at Retirement (add retirement values A and B)	_____	$1,442,902
Factor from Table 6.3 (example uses 25 years and 6% return)	_____	.056
Annual Retirement Income from Investments, Increasing at 3% per Year (multiply total value of investments by factor)	_____	$ 80,802
Social Security and Pensions	_____	$ 18,000
Total Retirement Income (increasing 3% per year)	_____	$ 98,802

FIGURE 6.1   Your Retirement Glide Path: Income Worksheet.

set aside for retirement, your 401(k), 403(b), 457 plans, plus any other investments you think of as retirement money. Then, add any money you're currently contributing plus any money your organization is contributing. With these items, simply fill in the worksheet. A full explanation of the steps of all the worksheets follows the example and worksheets.

The Example

Cecilia has been a computer programmer for 20 years; she is 45, and single. She is planning on retiring at 65, with 20 more years at programming, her career enjoyment. She owns a house, drives a convertible, and in general enjoys life.

	YOU	EXAMPLE
Salary now	_____	$85,000
Replacement ratio from Table 6.4	_____	64%
Retirement expenses	_____	54,400
Expenses that will *decrease*		
Mortgage	_____	15,000
Other	_____	0
Expenses that will *increase*		
Vacations	_____	5,000
Medical, Other	_____	5,000
Retirement expenses now (subtract and add amounts from Retirement Expenses)	_____ _____	49,400
Years to retirement	_____	20
Factor from Table 6.1 (example uses 3% inflation increases)	_____	1.81
Retirement expenses at retirement (multiply amount of expenses by factor)	_____	$89,414

FIGURE 6.2 Your Retirement Glide Path: Expense Worksheet.

She has accumulated $158,000 toward retirement mostly in her 401(k) plan at work. She is contributing 10 percent of her $85,000 salary to the plan along with her firm putting in an additional 4 percent. Her mortgage will be paid off in 15 years, so she'll have no mortgage expense when she retires.

The worksheet (see Figure 6.1 with factors derived from Tables 6.1 through 6.3) shows that she could have a retirement income at 65 of $98,802 (before taxes), counting $18,000 from Social Security. Her next step is to figure what

TABLE 6.1 Investment Returns or Inflation Increases (Growing a Lump Sum or Increasing Expenses)

	3%	4%	6%	8%	10%	12%
5 years	1.16	1.22	1.34	1.47	1.61	1.76
10 years	1.34	1.48	1.79	2.16	2.59	3.11
15 years	1.56	1.80	2.40	3.17	4.18	5.47
20 years	1.81	2.19	3.21	4.66	6.73	9.65
25 years	2.09	2.67	4.29	6.85	10.83	17.00
30 years	2.43	3.24	5.74	10.06	17.45	29.96

TABLE 6.2 Investment Returns (Annual Increasing Contributions)

	4%		6%		8%		10%		12%	
5 years	5.52	0%	5.81	0%	6.10	0%	6.41	0%	6.73	0%
	5.85	3%	6.14	3%	6.45	3%	6.77	3%	7.10	3%
	5.91	5%	6.38	5%	6.69	5%	7.02	5%	7.36	5%
10 years	12.25	0%	13.58	0%	15.07	0%	16.73	0%	18.60	0%
	13.91	3%	15.34	3%	16.95	3%	18.75	3%	20.75	3%
	14.38	5%	16.68	5%	18.37	5%	20.26	5%	22.37	5%
15 years	20.42	0%	23.97	0%	28.24	0%	33.36	0%	39.52	0%
	24.78	3%	28.79	3%	33.58	3%	39.29	3%	46.12	3%
	26.24	5%	32.72	5%	37.90	5%	44.06	5%	51.40	5%
20 years	30.37	0%	37.89	0%	47.59	0%	60.14	0%	76.38	0%
	39.27	3%	48.10	3%	59.38	3%	73.82	3%	92.34	3%
	42.57	5%	57.05	5%	69.60	5%	85.56	5%	105.89	5%
25 years	42.48	0%	56.51	0%	76.03	0%	103.26	0%	141.33	0%
	58.35	3%	75.47	3%	98.90	3%	131.11	3%	175.56	3%
	64.74	5%	93.27	5%	120.02	5%	156.42	5%	206.15	5%
30 years	57.21	0%	81.43	0%	117.81	0%	172.72	0%	255.81	0%
	83.25	3%	113.86	3%	158.82	3%	225.33	3%	324.27	3%
	94.52	5%	146.42	5%	199.01	5%	275.68	5%	388.23	5%

TABLE 6.3 Investment Returns (Withdrawing 3 Percent Increasing Amounts)

	4%	6%	8%	10%	12%
5 years	0.205	0.215	0.225	0.235	0.245
10 years	0.105	0.115	0.126	0.136	0.148
15 years	0.072	0.082	0.093	0.105	0.117
20 years	0.055	0.066	0.077	0.090	0.103
25 years	0.045	0.056	0.068	0.081	0.096
30 years	0.038	0.050	0.062	0.076	0.091
35 years	0.034	0.045	0.058	0.073	0.088
40 years	0.030	0.042	0.056	0.071	0.087

her expenses might be at retirement, the other side of the income/expense balancing act.

For the *expense worksheet* (Figure 6.2), she only needs her current salary and an estimate of how her expenses might change in retirement, less mortgage, increased vacations, and so forth. She used 64 percent for her replacement ratio from Table 6.4 for that. This is all shown in the worksheet. Her $85,000 salary (gross) is multiplied by 64 percent to obtain her targeted expenses of $54,400 ($85,000 times 0.64 equals $54,400). This $54,400 is also equal to her gross income needed in retirement to maintain her lifestyle if she retired today. We'll increase this in a moment to project the value to retirement 20 years ahead. First, we adjust any expenses that we can determine will increase or decrease. It's only a best guess at this point. Cecelia plans that her expenses should decrease overall by $5,000 a year. There would be a decrease of $15,000 for a mortgage that will be paid up by then, but a projected increase of $10,000 for additional vacation and medical expenses. Thus, her estimated expenses would be $49,400 if she retired today ($54,400 minus $5,000 equals $49,400).

Cecilia then projected this $49,400 to retirement 20 years from now. She consulted Table 6.1 for 20 years and found the factor of 1.81. This gives her an estimate of what her projected retirement expenses could be, or $89,414 ($49,400 times 1.81 equals $89,414).

She is now in a position to compare her projected annual retirement income of $98,802 to her projected retirement expenses of $89,414, giving her a measure of comfort. With this preliminary calculation showing her retirement income exceeding her expenses by about $10,000 a year, Cecilia appropriately feels that she's on a glide path to retirement at 65.

To be even more precise about her expenses, she completed the expense list at the end of Chapter 7 (see Figure 7.1). She listed what her retirement expenses would be if she retired now and obtained the total of $51,210. Because this is close to the $49,400 previously estimated, it's reasonable for her to have

TABLE 6.4 Replacement Ratios (for Couples or Singles)

Gross salary before retirement	$25,000	$35,000	$50,000	$75,000	$100,000
Replacement ratio	72%	70%	65%	64%	63%

confidence in her retirement glide path. She'll be repeating this worksheet several times between now and retirement, to make sure she stays on course.

Step-by-Step Worksheet Items

Now it's your turn. Complete the two worksheets and make a comparison between them to see how close you are to your retirement date. To help, here are some more comments and a discussion of each step in the worksheets.

Begin the Income Worksheet by totaling your investments that are designated for retirement. Typically these are 401(k)s, 403(b)s, 457s, IRAs, and other accounts. You may have other money for college expenses or a fund for a new car. Those don't count.

Use Table 6.1 to determine a factor for how much you'll have at retirement. For example, if you're 10 years away and you project that your investments will earn an overall 8 percent, then the factor is 2.16. Multiply your retirement money by this factor. That's how much you might have then. Redo this calculation every year or so to see if your investment amounts are on track.

Then determine how much you are contributing to your retirement funds. Is it taken from your paycheck? That's easier to determine than if you are sending money to your mutual fund account in varying amounts. If your organization is contributing to your plan, then add that, unless you won't be staying long enough for that money to vest.

Use Table 6.2 to determine a factor for how much you'll have at retirement. For example, if you're 10 years away, project that your investments will earn an overall 8 percent, and you'll increase the contributions by 3 percent a year (because your salary is increasing at that rate); then the factor is 16.95. Multiply your retirement money by this factor. That's how much your contributions and your organizations will have grown by then.

Adding these two numbers gives you an estimate of what your total investments could be at retirement. But we're not done. We can now convert that total into a potential retirement income stream. Use Table 6.3 for this purpose. It provides an estimate of the amount of annual income your investments could provide, with increases for inflation each year thereafter. Our assumptions begin with the generally accepted rule that we should plan our retirement to at least age 90—that gives us a planning horizon. If you retire at 65, that would give you a 25-year retirement.

The last aspect before you can determine the factor from Table 6.3 is what your expected investment return could be in retirement. If you determine that your investments have an asset allocation that's slightly less risky than when you're working because you want to be more conservative, then perhaps your investment return might be 6 percent or lower. The factor for 25 years and 6 percent investments is 0.056. Multiplying the total retirement investments by this factor results in the highest potential income stream from your investments.

If you were just planning on taking out the interest and dividend income or growth in your retirement portfolio, then you would multiply by that income and growth percentage. For example, if you had projected your retirement investments were $500,000 and you expected a 5 percent income and growth, you could expect to withdraw about $25,000 a year, keeping the principal intact.

Add your expected pensions and Social Security to this investment stream and you've determined your retirement income at retirement. You've now completed one-half of the retirement glide path worksheets.

The Expense Worksheet looks at the other side, your potential expenses at retirement. Start with your salary now (or your total salaries if married). Next apply the appropriate replacement ratio (Table 6.4). You'll see that the ratio is fairly constant at $50,000 or higher. Multiply your salary by this ratio. This gives you what your retirement expenses would be today.

What's behind the ratio? Generally it is a decrease in your total expenses. It's not that you'll spend less for everyday things, like groceries or eating out, but you'll notice a decrease in the taxes you pay and potentially a few other items. When we're no longer working, we don't pay the 7.65 percent FICA taxes. Also, Social Security payments could be taxed at only a fraction of regular taxes. Once retired, you no longer have to save for retirement. That's a decrease in your yearly outlays. Finally, your commuting costs, and often clothing expenses, will decrease once you've stopped working. Averaging all of these decreases results in a replacement ratio. You apply it to your gross salary to determine what your gross retirement income needs to be, on average, to maintain your lifestyle in retirement. For example, a person earning $50,000 would need about 65 percent, or $32,500 in gross income in retirement, on average, to continue the same lifestyle in retirement.

Next, identify the expenses that may decrease or increase once you retire. It may be that you would pay off your mortgage and increase your travel expenses. Also, you might calculate the decrease in expenses when your two teenagers leave home. Once you've accounted for these pluses and minuses, you have determined what your retirement expenses would be now, today.

The final step is to project this expense figure into the future to your retirement date. Use Table 6.1, generally under the 3 percent column, for the number of years from now to retirement. If you're 40 and are planning on retiring at age

60, then use the factor of 1.81. Multiply the retirement expenses today by that factor. This will result in your estimated annual expenses at retirement.

Now you're ready to compare the results from each worksheet. Compare your projected income with your projected expenses. If there is a surplus, then you should be on a glide path to retirement. If there is a shortfall, then you need to make adjustments, most often by moving retirement to a later date. Redo the worksheets with adjustments until you find that point where your projected income matches projected expenses. This is your new target. Redoing these worksheets every couple of years will allow you to keep your eye on your glide path and be able to better make adjustments as events in your job, life, or stock market call for changes.

Jillian and Jack

She was a busy executive who didn't want to believe that she had enough to retire. Ditto for Jack. Jillian and her husband were worried that they would have to just keep on working. At 53, they had accumulated $2 million and only needed an after-tax income of $120,000. They were hopeful that they could retire in just a few years at 55.

They didn't sit still for extensive worksheet planning, so I showed them a simple table I created at the behest of *Money* magazine many years ago. Several other publications, including *Time* magazine, have since used it because it is a quick way to get an answer to the affordability question.

Jillian and Jack had enough money, based on the table. Like many professional couples, who work and struggle for most of their adult lives to meet an attractive lifestyle, they had difficulty seeing that they just might have accumulated enough to actually retire. It's not that I was trying to get two more people to retire. Far from it. Jillian didn't want to retire and shouldn't, because she is still dedicated to her work, which forms a significant part of her life and her identity. The same is true for Jack.

However, it was beneficial to them to finally realize that they were working because they wanted to, not because they had to. Jillian and Jack now have a more positive attitude about their lives, and their work, and have significantly reduced their stress level. This example speaks to the question, if you've accumulated enough, do you want to continue to work, alter what you're doing, or simply call it quits?

Like Jillian and Jack, you can quickly check to see whether you'll have enough. Table 6.5 shows that for $2 million in retirement savings and investments, they

TABLE 6.5 Do You Have Enough?

RETIREMENT SAVINGS	AGES				
	50	55	60	62	65
$ 75,000	$ 8,400	$ 10,200	$ 12,700	$ 15,000	$ 17,000
100,000	9,850	11,700	14,000	17,000	18,900
150,000	12,700	14,500	17,500	20,000	22,000
250,000	18,500	20,800	24,000	26,900	29,000
500,000	33,000	35,900	40,000	43,000	46,500
750,000	47,500	51,000	56,000	60,000	64,000
1,000,000	62,000	66,000	72,000	76,000	81,000
2,000,000	120,000	126,000	136,000	142,000	150,000
3,000,000	177,000	187,000	200,000	208,000	220,000
5,000,000	293,000	308,000	328,000	340,000	358,000

could afford a lifestyle of $126,000 at age 55. The assumptions were that the $126,000 would increase 3 percent each year for inflation protection, their investments would increase at 8 percent per year, at age 62 they would collect their Social Security benefits, and there were no pensions available. The amount of money listed on the table is a gross figure, before payment of taxes.

If you've accumulated $1,000,000 by 62, you could afford a retirement of $76,000. Or, if you had $750,000 at age 65, you could afford $64,000.

A Final Word

Many people ask the following question, in one form or another: "If I can get an income of $35,000 [insert your number] a year, will that be enough to retire?" I usually give an equally general answer: "If you shop at Price Club it might be; if you frequent Lord & Taylor, then probably not."

Thus, projecting your finances to a specific retirement date carries a bag of assumptions. But that's all we've got in mid-career. So, make reasonable guesses about when you'll be able to retire, investment rates of return, and inflation, and then calculate your glide path to retirement.

CHAPTER 7

Good News and Bad News for Boomers

In 1976, the tuition at the University of Pennsylvania was $3,790; today it's $23,254, a 5.1-fold increase. But the cost of living is only up 2.9-fold since then. So, if it seems that some things cost more today, you're right.

Today, we need a wireless phone, cable TV, Internet-connected computer, microwave oven, Walkman, and . . . caffe latte with vanilla flavoring. None of these things were around for our parents. So, if you think you buy more stuff today, you're right.

Now people work on average 3.5 hours more in their main job than they did in 1977, so if you think you work more, you're right. We also spend more time commuting to work. Some actually spend an astounding hour or more each way, to and from work, every day; so, if it seems as if you have less personal time, you're right.

Life expectancy is also inflated. We're living 15 years longer than when Social Security was created. Which means we have 15 more years to buy more stuff.

The good news is that we have actually increased our standard of living, no trivial economic feat. But, like all progress, it comes with a price. The bad news is that we work more, spend more, and, on average, save less. The bottom line: Retirement will be more expensive and more difficult to attain.

Actually, because of the extraordinary bull market in the 1980s and 1990s, especially the 1995 to 1999 period, many boomers made considerable money in the stock market, boosting their retirement nest eggs. Yes, some portfolios were recently scorched, bad news for those boomers. But many didn't reach for that risk and have kept their market gains largely intact. Thus, investments for many boomers have made retirement more attainable.

While some boomers have saved and successfully invested, others have not. Surveys show that a considerable number of boomers have, on average, only $1,000 in savings. Obviously, many boomers will not be able to retire until later in life, perhaps not until age 70 or 75.

Headlines Don't Help

Have you seen the occasional article or book proclaiming that once the baby boomers retire all hell will break loose? The stock market will tank, real estate values will fall off a cliff, and in general, life as we know it in the Western world will cease to exist.

The argument goes like this: When the 78 million boomers leave the workforce they will unload their equities, sell their large 4-bedroom, 2-garage, 3-bathroom duplex, and head for some sun-soaked piece of heaven. This will cause the value of stocks and real estate to plummet.

The attitude behind those articles is more worrisome than the actual prospects of it happening. It is worrisome because people may actually believe it, like the millennium catastrophe that never happened.

When I confront someone who believes this scary scenario, I usually pose a few questions: "Will boomers all retire on the same day, or even the same week?" The response is something like, "Well, obviously, no." Boomers like other generations are scattered over 18 years and will retire gradually over many years. And, just maybe, at the same time the GenX and GenY folks will be busy building up their portfolios and buying real estate.

Then I ask: "Do you think the boomers, who have fallen in love with stocks, are simply going to abandon them? Sell them and squirrel their money in boring CDs?" "Well, now that you mention it, probably not." In other words, when we hear this doomsday scenario, we should be more than a little skeptical.

Having been weaned on stocks, boomers will keep a significant portion of their portfolios in individual stocks or mutual funds. The stock market should be just fine. And, I doubt that most boomers will pick up and move to some boring shuffle-board retirement village in greater numbers than their parents. And GenX and GenY folks will be busy as ever buying real estate. The housing market should flourish as well.

Some Recent History

The press, too, has been whipsawed by the market. Before the great surge in the market, the *Wall Street Journal* (June 5, 1995) blared on its front page, "Many Baby Boomers Save Little, May Run into Trouble Later On." That same year, *Time* magazine (March 20, 1995) trumpeted a cover story, "The Case for Killing Social Security." The *New York Times* (March 26, 1995) in a lead Business Section article declared "Another Day Older and Running Out of Time," with the subheadline "For Retirement, Americans Say They're More Scared than Prepared." The *New Republic* (July 17, 24, 1995) carried an article titled "Why Americans Don't Save." A *Fortune* magazine (September 11, 1995) cover story asked "Will You Be Able to Retire?" and later the *Wall Street Journal* (May 6, 1996) in the front page Outlook Section proclaimed, "Early Retirement Isn't in the Boomers' Future."

Starting in late 1996, after the market had already turned upward for a year, sentiment changed and articles began to offer outright optimism for retirement. *Money* magazine's (October 1996) front page teased with "Retire with All the Money You'll Ever Need," *Fortune* (October 27, 1997) countered with "How to Win at Retirement," *Smart Money*'s (November 1997) headline read "Retire Ten Years Early," and on a later cover, *Money* (November 1997) recommended "Save Wisely and Retire Rich."

What's right? Is retirement a formidable goal or an easy one? Paradoxically, in fact, it's both. Retirement will increasingly offer a wide array of outcomes—some people will actually be able to retire early, while others will struggle to retire even at age 70 or 75. Some are building up pensions, 401(k)s, and personal savings, while others have none.

So, the bottom line for boomers is, retirement will be a more divergent event than for their parents.

How to Deal with Inflation

In the past couple of years, the CPI (Consumer Price Index) has been quietly adjusted. It now considers that people do change their buying habits if prices go up. If meat is high, consumers may move to fish or pasta. Also, the CPI now considers that some consumers buy at discount, warehouse, and outlet stores, where savings can be significant.

What is the CPI? It's the official monthly attempt to quantify how much more it costs to buy stuff this month than last, a general cost-of-living indicator. Of course, we don't all buy the same things, so how can the CPI represent you? It can't; it can only give a general average. However, it's the best guess we have, and it's probably a good estimate for most of us.

The good news for retirees is that the cost of living in retirement is generally lower than the monthly CPI figures. Not a whole lot, but generally slightly less. My own anecdotal evidence with clients from the mid-1980s to the present reflects this. The CPI figures have generally shown inflation of 3 percent a year, whereas my retired clients have shown only 1 percent to 2 percent.

Why? Most people have their housing established, furniture bought, and in general don't need to buy the larger and more costly items like refrigerators, lawn mowers, and so forth.

Actually our individual cost of living throughout our lives is not a simple linear increase year by year (Table 7.1). When people begin their careers, they drastically increase their lifestyle within 5 to 10 years to a degree that no CPI could capture. From trying, at first, to make ends meet by sharing an apartment, to having one's own apartment; next perhaps getting married and moving into a condo or house; and then having to buy furniture to fill the rooms—the progression comprises a quantum leap in expenses. Once people are established in mid-career, the official CPI may come close to reflecting reality.

Suggestion: Using 3 percent for inflation projections will give you a cushion in your retirement planning. Conservative planning is generally the best approach. If inflation picks up and starts to average higher, say, 4 percent or higher, then you'll need to adjust your projections accordingly.

Estimating Retirement Expenses

You're 10 to 20 years away from retirement, so how can you estimate your expenses when you retire? First, try to estimate what those expenses would be if you were retired today. Why today? Because you have a feel for what things cost today. Next, project those expenses referring back to Table 6.1. That will give you a feel for what your expenses will be at retirement.

TABLE 7.1 Inflation Year by Year

Annual Rates of Inflation from 1960 through 2000

YEAR	INFLATION (%)	YEAR	INFLATION (%)
1960	1.48	1970	5.49
1961	0.67	1971	3.36
1962	1.22	1972	3.41
1963	1.65	1973	8.80
1964	1.19	1974	12.20
1965	1.92	1975	7.01
1966	3.35	1976	4.81
1967	3.04	1977	6.77
1968	4.72	1978	9.03
1969	6.11	1979	13.31
Average	2.5		7.4
1980	12.40	1990	6.11
1981	8.94	1991	3.06
1982	3.87	1992	2.90
1983	3.80	1993	2.75
1984	3.95	1994	2.67
1985	3.77	1995	2.54
1986	1.13	1996	3.32
1987	4.41	1997	1.70
1988	4.42	1998	1.61
1989	4.65	1999	2.68
Average	5.1		2.9
		2000	3.86

Source: Bureau of Labor Statistics.

Note: Average 1960–2000: 4.5%

Range of inflation 1960–2000: 0.67% to 13.31%

Average 1926–2000: 3.1%

Date: _____

	CURRENT EXPENSES	RETIREMENT EXPENSES
HOUSING		
Rent		
Mortgage	$15,000	$ 0–
Property taxes	3,700	3,700
Utilities (gas/oil/electric/water)	2,000	2,000
Telephone	600	600
Household maintenance (lawn/etc.)	1,000	1,000
Household help	0	0
Other (furniture/other)	250	250
CLOTHING (purchases/cleaning)	1,800	1,800
FOOD (groceries)	4,500	4,500
TRANSPORTATION		
Purchase of auto (annual outlay)	5,500	5,500
Repairs and maintenance	350	350
Gas and oil	1,100	1,100
Other (commuting/taxis/parking)	100	100
ENTERTAINMENT		
Vacations	1,000	6,000+
Dining out	1,800	2,800+
Movies and plays	200	200
Parties	300	1,300+
Sports and hobbies	350	1,350+
Other (cable TV)	450	450
EDUCATION (tuition/books/supplies)	1,200	1,200
GIFTS (holidays/birthdays)	1,000	1,000
CONTRIBUTIONS	750	750
LOANS (education/auto)	0	0
CHILD CARE (day care, baby sitters)	0	0
PERSONAL ITEMS		
Barber and beauty shop	250	250
Cigarettes and tobacco	0	0
Toiletries and cosmetics	350	350
Pet food and supplies	200	200
MEDICAL (doctors/medications)	2,000	2,000
INSURANCE PREMIUMS		
Life	0	0
Medical	500	2,500+
Disability	0	0
Auto	800	800
Property and liability	250	250
OTHER (legal, tax, financial, other)	750	750
Basic Living Expenses	**$48,050**	**$43,050**

FIGURE 7.1 Estimated Annual Expenses—Example.

INCOME TAXES		
Federal	14,500	6,800
FICA (Social Security tax)*	5,850	0
State income taxes	3,100	1,360
Total Income Taxes	$23,450	$ 8,160
SAVINGS AND INVESTMENTS		
Payroll savings (401(k)/other)	8,500	0
IRAs, SEPs, and Keoghs	0	0
Other savings and investments	0	0
Total Expenses	$85,000	$51,210

Note: + or − next to the right column denotes a change, plus or minus.

* FICA rate in 2001 is 7.65 percent up to $80,400 and continuing at 1.45 percent over $80,400.

FIGURE 7.1 (Continued)

To estimate today's costs, study the example shown in Figure 7.1 and then complete the expense worksheet (Figure 7.2) at the end of this chapter. Then add and subtract items that should change by the time you start retirement. Maybe you will have your mortgage paid for. You may have children at home now and/or are paying their college expenses. If those costs will end by retirement, adjust your figures accordingly. You can also adjust categories like clothing and groceries for the kids. Some costs may go the other way, such as increased vacations and entertainment.

Finally, project those expenses as was shown in Chapter 6 using Table 6.1. If you estimate that your retirement expenses today would be $55,000 and you plan to retire in 15 years, then using the 3 percent column in Table 6.1, the factor is 1.56. Multiplying $55,000 by 1.56 equals $85,800. That would be an estimate of your first year's retirement expenses.

The caveat is that you could change your lifestyle between now and retirement. So, how do you account for that? You plan conservatively and you recalculate your expenses every couple of years to see if you need to adjust your plan.

List of Expenses

Figure 7.1 is a sample worksheet of expenses. They are for Cecilia, the example used in Chapter 6. Figure 7.2 provides a worksheet that you can complete.

Date: _____

	CURRENT EXPENSES	RETIREMENT EXPENSES
HOUSING		
Rent	_____	_____
Mortgage	_____	_____
Property taxes	_____	_____
Utilities (gas/oil/electric/water)	_____	_____
Telephone	_____	_____
Household maintenance (lawn/etc.)	_____	_____
Household help	_____	_____
Other (furniture/other)	_____	_____
CLOTHING (purchases/cleaning)	_____	_____
FOODS (groceries)	_____	_____
TRANSPORTATION		
Purchase of auto (annual outlay)	_____	_____
Repairs and maintenance	_____	_____
Gas and oil	_____	_____
Other (commuting/taxis/parking)	_____	_____
ENTERTAINMENT		
Vacations	_____	_____
Dining out	_____	_____
Movies and plays	_____	_____
Parties	_____	_____
Sports and hobbies	_____	_____
Other (cable TV)	_____	_____
EDUCATION (tuition/books/supplies)	_____	_____
GIFTS (holidays/birthdays)	_____	_____
CONTRIBUTIONS	_____	_____
LOANS (education/auto)	_____	_____
CHILD CARE (day care, baby sitters)	_____	_____
PERSONAL ITEMS		
Barber and beauty shop	_____	_____
Cigarettes and tobacco	_____	_____
Toiletries and cosmetics	_____	_____
Pet food and supplies	_____	_____
MEDICAL (doctors/medications)	_____	_____
INSURANCE PREMIUMS		
Life	_____	_____
Medical	_____	_____
Disability	_____	_____
Auto	_____	_____
Property and liability	_____	_____
OTHER (special items/other)	_____	_____
Basic Living Expenses	$ _____	$ _____

FIGURE 7.2 Estimated Annual Expenses.

INCOME TAXES
    Federal
    FICA (Social Security tax)*
    State income taxes
        Total Income Taxes $ _____ $ _____

SAVINGS AND INVESTMENTS
    Payroll savings (401(k)/other)
    IRAs, SEPs, and Keoghs
    Other savings and investments
        Total Expenses $ _____ $ _____

Note: + or − next to the right column denotes a change, plus or minus.

* FICA rate in 2001 is 7.65 percent up to $80,400 and continuing at 1.45 percent over $80,400.

FIGURE 7.2 (Continued)

CHAPTER 8

Social Security Insecurity

You will get Social Security. I guarantee it. Don't believe the naysayers who point to declining numbers that show only 3.3 current workers paying into the system for every person receiving a benefit. Yes, in 1950 it was 16.5 workers to every beneficiary and in 2025 it will be only 2 workers per beneficiary. But, we'll somehow solve this problem.

Here's my logic. After you've paid a lifetime of FICA taxes into the system, do you think the government could say to you: "Sorry, but we don't have enough to pay your benefit." You and millions of other Americans would repeat 1776 and form a new government.

The only questions are: How much will you get and will it be from our current pay-as-we-go transfer payment system, or will it be from a new form that includes individual investment accounts?

Tax Highlight

SOCIAL SECURITY CHANGES

2000 Elimination of Social Security earnings test at 65, or full retirement age.

2001–2002 Social Security earnings test for year of 65, or full retirement, is $25,000 in 2001, $30,000 in 2002.

The first Social Security recipient was Ida Mae Fuller in 1940. Her benefit was $22.45 per month. She lived until she just turned 100, collecting about $20,000 in benefits—for her $22 in contributions. Today, an expanded system offers a substantial benefit. For example, the maximum benefit in 2001 at age 65 is around $17,500 a year, with an average benefit of about $11,800. The maximum earner could now receive over $350,000 if he or she lives until 85, the average earner $236,000.

You now receive a yearly estimate from Social Security, or you can order one by calling their phone number. You can also ask questions and get recorded information:

800-SSA-1213

With the estimate, you'll get a history of your earnings (up to the maximum each year) and an estimate of your benefit at 62 and 65. For a generalized amount, see Table 8.1.

For more information on Social Security, you can also go to their official Web site. Once there, you can also get an estimate of your benefit:

www.ssa.gov

Calculating Social Security

But Social Security is more than a retirement benefit, it includes spouse's and survivor benefits, disability for workers at all ages, and medical benefits for those over 65.

A spouse's benefit was initially put into the system to recognize women's time raising families and not earning a salary, although today the spouse's

TABLE 8.1 Estimates of Annual Social Security Benefits

	MAXIMUM EARNER (CURRENTLY $80,400)	AVERAGE EARNER (CURRENTLY $35,000)
2005	$22,000	$15,000
2010	28,000	18,000
2015	35,000	22,000
2020	44,000	28,000

The Six Steps for Determining Your Social Security Benefit

1. Essentially all working years are included in the calculation. Most people assume it's like a pension, using only the last 5 or 10 years. Actually 35 years must be used. If a person only worked for 20 years then the remaining 15 years are calculated as zero.

2. All salary and wages up to the maximum each year are used for the calculation. For example, in 2001 the maximum salary on which FICA taxes are paid is $80,400. If you are over that amount, then you continue to pay 1.45 percent for Medicare Part A, but none of it is used for this calculation.

3. Past years of salary are boosted upward by an increase in average wages. This gives salaries in early career years a higher value than actual salaries.

4. The highest 35 years are then averaged. This results in an average annual salary that's used in the formula described next.

5. This is the critical step in the calculation, where different percentages are applied to the value attained in Step 4. In 2001, the first 90 percent of $6,732 is added to 32 percent of the next $33,840, and 15 percent over $40,572 (if available). Adding these amounts determines the basic benefit. (The numbers $6,732 and $40,572 are called bend points.)

6. Cost-of-living increases are applied to benefits over age 62, and voilà, a final benefit is determined.

benefit is nongender. The benefit is as much as 50 percent of worker's benefit if started at 65. There is a 25 percent reduction if taken at 62.

A survivor's benefit recognizes the totality of a couple's Social Security benefit by allowing a spouse to receive 100 percent of the worker's benefit at 65. The benefit can start as early as 60, but is reduced to 71.5 percent at that age.

Social Security will calculate any and all benefits you could be entitled to, your own, a spouses, or a survivor benefit. You receive the highest benefit.

Three complicated aspects of the system involve: When will you get your full benefit, how is it taxed, and how is your benefit affected if you earn money.

Your Full Retirement Age

Yes, younger workers will have to wait longer than 65 to receive a full benefit. You will still be able to start your benefit at age 62, but it will be further reduced. Table 8.2 summarizes these new ages.

How a Benefit Is Taxed

Once you receive a benefit, it could be taxed. Figuring the tax is a little complicated, so a worksheet is provided in the 1040 tax instruction booklet and duplicated below (see Figure 8.1). Essentially, if you are single and your income is less than $25,000 or married and your income is less than $32,000, then your Social Security benefit is not taxed at all. If you exceed these amounts, up to 50 percent of the benefit can be taxed. If you exceed the further amounts of $34,000 if single, $44,000 if married, then as much as 85 percent can be taxed.

That doesn't mean that the tax rate is 85 percent, it means that up to 85 percent of the benefit is taxed at whatever tax rate bracket you're in. As an example,

TABLE 8.2 Full Retirement Age

YEAR OF BIRTH	
1938	65 plus 2 months
1939	65 plus 4 months
1940	65 plus 6 months
1941	65 plus 8 months
1942	65 plus 10 months
1943–1954	66
1955	66 plus 2 months
1956	66 plus 4 months
1957	66 plus 6 months
1958	66 plus 8 months
1959	66 plus 10 months
1960 and later	67

(From the actual worksheet in the Form 1040 instruction booklet, including the lines from the 2000 version of Form 1040)

	YOU	EXAMPLE
1. Enter Social Security benefit(s)	_____	$25,000
2. Enter one-half of Social Security	_____	12,500
3. Add all income (lines 7–21), but *not* line 8a (tax exempt) and *not* Social Security (line 20)	_____	21,000
4. Enter line 8a (tax exempt interest)	_____	0
5. Add lines 2, 3 and 4	_____	33,500
6. Enter lines 23–31, but not line 24 (student loan interest)	_____	0
7. Subtract line 6 from 5		33,500
8. Enter $25,000 if single, $32,000 if married, $0 if married filing separately	_____	32,000
9. Subtract line 8 from 7 (stop if zero or less— none of your Social Security is taxed)	_____	1,500
10. Enter $9,000 if single, $12,000 if married, $0 if married filing separately		12,000
11. Subtract line 10 from 9, if less than zero, enter zero	_____	0
12. Enter the smaller of line 9 or 10	_____	1,500
13. Enter one-half of line 12	_____	750
14. Enter the smaller of line 2 or 13	_____	750
15. Multiply line 11 by 85% (0.85)	_____	0
16. Add lines 14 and 15	_____	750
17. Multiply line 1 by 0.85	_____	21,250
18. Enter the smaller of line 16 or 17 (This is the taxable amount of Social Security— enter on line 20b of the 2000 version of Form 1040)	_____	$ 750

FIGURE 8.1 Social Security Taxation Worksheet.

using the worksheet shown in Figure 8.1, Rob and Sheila have a total retirement income of $46,000, comprising pension and investment income of $21,000 and Social Security of $25,000. In completing the form, they determined that only $750 of their Social Security will be taxed. Since they're in the 28 percent federal tax bracket, they will pay only $210 in taxes on their $25,000 Social Security ($750 times .28 equals $210). Most states exempt Social Security from taxation.

What If You Earn Money while Collecting a Benefit?

As a holdover from the Depression days, when Social Security was created, there is still an earnings test. This means that some of your benefits may be reduced if you work. However, if you're over 65 (or your full retirement age) then none of your benefit will be reduced regardless of any earnings. Earnings only include wages and net self-employment earnings, not pensions, interest, or capital gains.

If you're collecting a benefit and are 62 through 64, then in 2001, your benefit will be reduced $1 for every $2 of earnings over $10,680. For instance, if you earned $12,000, which exceeds the limit by $1,320, then your benefit will be reduced by $660 in 2001 ($1,320 times 0.5 equals $660).

Making this calculation even more complicated, but beneficial, there is now a higher limit for the year in which you turn 65 (or your full retirement age), up to the actual date when you turn 65. In 2001, if you earn less than $25,000 before you turn 65, and in 2002 less than $30,000, then you keep all of your benefit that year.

What to do? If your earnings are considerably above the earnings test, don't collect any benefit—defer it. It could be mostly eliminated by the test. By deferring the benefit to a later date or age 65 (or your full retirement age), your benefit will probably be larger because of the deferral and additional earnings.

What's the Future?

Looming is an arithmetic that cannot be avoided. By 2015, the payroll tax alone will no longer be sufficient to pay for all the benefits. At that time, we'll have to deal with the shortfall in one of several ways: increased payroll taxes, reduced benefits, or a combination of both. President Bush has proposed individual accounts to help deal with this shortfall. The following section explains my own suggestion, which includes these accounts. It's from an opinion piece I did in August 1999 for the *Journal of Financial Planning*.

What If Social Security Were My Client?

Seeing the muddle on both sides of the political aisle on Social Security, I wondered, would it be helpful to come up with a comprehensive solution to the problems of Social Security from a financial and retirement planning point of view?

To make it easy for myself, I imagined that Social Security came to me as a retirement planning client. How would I advise it? I imagined that after a lengthy discussion about growing up in the Depression, making it big in the 1950s and 1960s, having a midlife crisis in the early 1980s, and even after the recent boom years, Social Security finally admitted that, alas, it still hasn't saved a penny for the future.

During our discussion, it was perhaps clearer why politicians have had difficulty with a solution. Over the years, the system has developed two very different purposes from the viewpoints of recipients and politicians.

The immediate purpose of Social Security, created during the Depression of the 1930s, was to provide a general safety net for the elderly. Even today, about one-half of the recipients rely on Social Security for most of their income. This half of recipients would be in poverty, or close to it, were it not for the system.

On the other hand, Social Security has become a financial base for millions of retirees, added to by personal savings and investments, 401(k) plans, and pensions.

To pay for these retirement benefits, we give Social Security 5.3 percent of our total FICA payroll tax of 7.65 percent, up to $80,400 in 2001. The rest of our contributions are for disability, 0.9 percent, and Medicare Part A, 1.45 percent. Our employer pays an equal amount as well; or for retirement purposes an amount equal to 10.6 percent, goes to pay for those currently on Social Security.

Long term, however, my hypothetical client emphasized, the 10.6 percent will provide only 75 percent of what will be needed to pay for the presently promised payments. Thus, the crux of the problem of Social Security is this 25 percent shortfall each year. So that's why Democrats and Republicans cringe about the future of the system. We're back to annual billion-dollar deficits as far as the eye can see!

"But I thought the Trustees just announced that the system was secure to year 2035," I volunteered, knowing the answer. "There are only IOUs, you see," my client sheepishly replied, "there is no actual money set aside, only promises that the government will somehow pay for them. Actually starting in 2015, or thereabouts, those government promises have to be made good, because beginning then FICA taxes alone cannot pay for all the benefits."

"Government promises are pretty good," I said. "Government can find money one way or another, either by increasing taxes, cutting back on other government programs, cutting back on Social Security benefits, or some of each. We'll find a way to get the money, won't we?"

"But none of this is assured," my client replied, "in fact two crucial problems are standing in the way. First, the public wants their benefits without paying any more for them—and the politicians want to oblige them. Second, the politicians want the other side of the aisle to propose the tough choices, so Social Security is available as a campaign issue. What I need is a plan from a nonpolitical source that addresses these interests."

That was my task. And, after considerable calculations and contemplations, I came up with a plan. Two criteria formed the basis of my approach: (1) The system should be put on a self-sustaining financial basis so workers will have confidence that they will get their promised benefits, and (2) workers should have the option of either investing their FICA contributions in the stock market or staying in the present system if they so choose.

Social Security was waiting breathlessly. I prefaced my plan, however, with this proviso: *Whatever I recommend, compare it to what will happen if nothing is changed:* deficits of billions of dollars each year. And for starters, it's assumed that those already on Social Security will not be affected.

Here is my plan:

1. Because there are two purposes, I recommend splitting the system in two and meeting each head-on. Use the *employer's 5.3 percent* to *fund the safety net,* available to those who have little or no financial means. Maintain that benefit as it is today with increases in cost of living, and if additional money is necessary, then fund it from general revenues (even today most of Medicare Part B is paid out of general revenues).

2. For the regular part, the financial base, give workers the option (a) of continuing with the current system with a phased-in decrease of 1 percent per year depending on one's age to an ultimate 25 percent decrease for the youngest workers, or (b) of investing FICA money in outside individual investment accounts.

3. Thus, those workers who feel comfortable with the current system, or are close to retirement, can continue to have guaranteed spousal and survivor benefits, payments for as long as they live, full benefits at age 65 (or their full retirement age) and early benefits at age 62, and cost-of-living increases. (Remember these are the non-safety-net workers.) To keep the system in balance on a long-term basis, benefits will decrease slowly, depending on age, 1 percent a year until benefits for the youngest workers reach the full decrease at the 25 percent level. As a financial adviser, I

want to get the system to a pay-as-we-can-afford-it basis. A benefit of $12,000 would be $11,880 after only a 1 percent decrease for the oldest affected workers. Today's maximum benefit of about $17,500 would be about $13,125 after the full 25 percent decrease for the youngest workers. Most important, from a retirement planning point of view, young people could then gain confidence in the system because it would be in financial balance as far as the eye can see.

4. As a financial planner, I see the potential for the stock market to provide an even more attractive benefit; thus, workers should be allowed to opt out of the present system by investing their FICA money in outside investment accounts. The amount that could be shifted to outside accounts would begin at 1 percent, so as not to disrupt the present system, and be allowed to increase in increments to eventually reach the full 5.3 percent. To keep a lid on account expenses, challenge the investment community, and keep the investments straightforward; only one-half of a percent would be allowed for fund expenses. Also, no commissions, 12b-1 (a marketing fee), and no back-end fees would be permitted. A $50 start-up fee would be allowed, with a $100 fee for transferring to another provider. Importantly, there would only be three types of investments: all equity, balanced (50 percent stocks and 50 percent bonds), and money market accounts. A worker could select any combination of these three options. The resultant benefit could be as great as twice what the benefit would be under current law.

5. If these individual accounts are selected, then anytime after age 62, individuals could begin their benefit, payable only as monthly payments (annuity payments) based on the amount of money in the account, with actuaries determining the annuity factors.

6. Do not allow the government to invest any money directly in the market. It would eventually be tainted by political influence and adversely affect the market. The most trusted and respected financial expert around, Alan Greenspan, is warning against this approach, and that should be enough to put this bad idea to rest.

"It sounds like a fine plan," my client said. "It offers a Social Security system attuned to today's world and includes the main concerns people and politicians have including the ability for workers and their financial planners to actually project a benefit with some confidence. Now I have to try to get it adopted."

I offered this counsel, "Tell the politicians and the people, if you can find a more sensible solution, great; but until then be admonished, the longer you wait, the longer you are being dishonest with young people who will have to endure the eventual changes to the system."

Finally, be comforted, a little, by how the last crisis was resolved. In 1982, Social Security was at a crossroads and the Democrats and Republicans couldn't resolve the problem on their own. A strong-willed Alan Greenspan headed a bipartisan commission and created a solution, which Congress and the President approved.

CHAPTER 9

Just How Long Will You Live?

An important part of your retirement equation is: "How long will I live?" In 1789, the first year George Washington took office, the average life expectancy was about 45. That is, at the time of our nation's founding, a newborn could only expect to live to what we regard today as early middle age.

A century later by 1900, life expectancy had only climbed to 47, a slight increase. Now, another century later with myriad medical advances, a newborn can expect to live to age 76—an increase of 62 percent from 1900 and an increase of about 69 percent from 1789. It seems hard to imagine that in Washington's time, life was already over in what we consider our prime. We live two lifetimes today compared with our founding fathers' one. In fact, historical actuaries have estimated that from the Bronze Age through to George Washington, life expectancy stayed at about age 45.

When Social Security came into being in 1935, the average life expectancy was 65. Today it is 15 years longer. So, if younger people have to wait until age 70 or later to retire, they're still ahead, at least on paper.

Tax Highlight

As of 2001 New life expectancy table for age 70½ minimum withdrawal rules for IRAs, 401(k)s, 403(b)s, 457s, and pensions. New simplified rules as well.

So, how long should you plan to live in retirement? Financial planners, who don't want their clients to outlive their money, commonly use age 90. It's a nice round number and it should be sufficient for planning purposes. You can use the life expectancy table shown in Table 9.1 for your own planning. Note the two sets of columns titled *50%* and *85%*. First look under the column for an age now, say age 60. Under the 50 percent columns for male and female, the table shows a life expectancy of 81 for men and 86 for women. It means that, on average (or there is a 50 percent chance), you'll live to this age. It also means that you have a 50 percent chance of not living to 81 or 86.

Let's stop for a moment. So, for retirement planning purposes, should you assume just 81 or 86? No. As my former colleague retired chief actuary Douglas C. Barton of Buck Consultants points out, using age 81 or 86 creates a false sense of security because you have a 50 percent chance of living longer! Thus, for prudent planning, you want to plan longer because you don't want to outlive your money. That's why financial planners have settled on age 90, and it appears to be an appropriate number.

Continue reading the table. Look under the 85 percent columns for age 60. It shows 91 for men and 96 for women. That means, if you lived longer than 85 percent of those in your age group, you would live to those ages. Or, you would be among the elite 15 percent in your age group who survived this long. Either way, it would be an additional 10 years. You probably know of people either first- or secondhand who have lived or are living in their 90s.

TABLE 9.1 Your Life Expectancy Table

AGE NOW	MALE		FEMALE	
	50%	85%	50%	85%
30	79	90	85	96
40	80	90	85	96
50	80	90	85	96
60	81	91	86	96
70	83	92	87	97
80	87	94	90	98
90	94	100	95	101

Source: 1985 Proceedings of the Conference of Actuaries in Public Practice.

To explain this particular table further, it's constructed from a population of people who work for larger organizations. People in this category, in general, are better educated and have better medical benefits, both correlated to longer lives. It's assumed that they have less dangerous lifestyles and seek more medical attention. In other words, it's a table for those who would probably buy a book on retirement planning, like you. (The table is from a published table in the 1985 *Proceedings of the Conference of Actuaries in Public Practice*.)

How Does Life Expectancy Change over Your Lifetime?

Let's return to our life expectancy table. For ages younger than 60, life expectancy doesn't change very much. In fact, at age 30, 40, or 50 there is about the same expectancy—from 79 to 80 for men and 85 for women. In other words, most people at work have about the same life expectancy.

If you live longer than 60, however, then your life expectancy begins to increase. As an example, the table shows that if you make it to age 80, then your average life expectancy has increased to 87 and 90. As actuaries say, "The longer you live, the longer you live." You've simply been heartier and luckier in avoiding accidents and diseases and are in a "survivor" category. Another facet of life expectancy is in the first few years after birth. Most are aware that the first years are more perilous to life. If you survive those very early years, then you have a reasonable probability to have a long life. But when you add those perilous years you get an overall lower life expectancy. Table 9.2 shows selected years with life expectancies from birth.

TABLE 9.2 Life Expectancy at Birth

	MALE	FEMALE	AVERAGE
1997	73.8	79.4	76.5
1980	70.0	77.5	73.7
1950	65.6	71.1	68.2
1940	60.8	65.2	62.9
1920	53.8	54.5	54.1
1900	46.3	48.3	47.3

Source: U.S. National Center for Health Statistics.

Why Do Women Outlive Men?

I've heard many casual reasons why women seem to be the heartier sex, ranging from "Men have it easier because they don't have to take care of the kids" to "Women live longer so they can take care of men." Actually, it appears to be a genetic trait. Women, on average, have lived and will probably continue to live longer than men. Next time you're in a nursing home, you'll observe that there are more women than men.

A significant planning implication for women is that they are most likely to be single at the end of their lives. They need to make sure that they have the financial resources and financial know-how for this extra time. Women are waking up to this realization, which is perhaps why more and more women are interested in finance.

What about Your Family Genes?

Should you, or can you, for planning purposes, alter average life expectancy numbers depending on your family's or your individual medical history? Probably not yet. We are making medical progress, so maybe this will change in the future. You may even know of people who were seemingly healthy, but died at a young age. A client who had medical problems was appropriately concerned about his healthy wife. He wanted to make sure she had enough money to last her for many retirement years. She died several years before he did. Medical history would have predicted it wouldn't happen.

Thus, medical science has not yet been able to bring much precision to retirement planning by adding or subtracting years from life expectancy numbers given medical conditions. So you're back to using either the generalized age 90 or older for your planning. If you're optimistic or just want to make absolutely sure you won't outlive your money, then you might want to pick a number between 90 and 100.

The IRS Tables for IRAs

If you have dealt with the age 70½ rules for IRAs and benefit plans, you have been rightfully confused. The rules were too complex. But, happily, the rules have been simplified as of 2001. It was actually not the new tax law that changed these rules; it was the IRS that issued proposed rules early in 2001.

Importantly, Table 9.3 now is to be used for this purpose. (It's actually a life expectancy table constructed with a joint expectancy of a person age 70 and a person 10 years younger.) This gives a larger life expectancy number resulting in a lower amount that must be taken from the IRAs.

Although Chapter 14 discusses in some detail how to do the calculation and the associated rules, let's use Table 9.3 so you can know in general how the minimum calculation is performed. Let's say the value of all of your IRAs at the beginning of the year totaled $150,000 and you were going to be age 70 (in the year you'll turn age 70½). The table shows the divisor of 26.2 for age 70. Simply divide the amount in the IRAs by the divisor to get $5,725 ($150,000 divided by 26.2 equals $5,725). That's the required minimum distribution for the year and must be taken or have a 50 percent penalty imposed on what you should have

TABLE 9.3 Individual Retirement Account—Age 70½—Divisor Table

AGE	DIVISOR	AGE	DIVISOR	AGE	DIVISOR
70	26.2	85	13.8	100	5.7
71	25.3	86	13.1	101	5.3
72	24.4	87	12.4	102	5.0
73	23.5	88	11.8	103	4.7
74	22.7	89	11.1	104	4.4
75	21.8	90	10.5	105	4.1
76	20.9	91	9.9	106	3.8
77	20.1	92	9.4	107	3.6
78	19.2	93	8.8	108	3.3
79	18.4	94	8.3	109	3.1
80	17.6	95	7.8	110	2.8
81	16.8	96	7.3	111	2.6
82	16.0	97	6.9	112	2.4
83	15.3	98	6.5	113	2.2
84	14.5	99	6.1	114	2.0
				115 and older	1.8

Source: IRS Publication 590.

taken. You can take more, but you must at least take this amount. Each year beginning at 70½ you perform this calculation to determine how much you must take out. Next year, you again determine the value of your IRAs and divide by the next year's number, or 25.3.

Although this table is for singles or marrieds, it is constructed with life expectancies of a worker who is married to a spouse 10 years younger. It results in a smaller amount that needs to be taken at 70½ and later years from IRAs and benefit plans. The only exception is for workers who are married to spouses who are greater than 10 years apart. They can consult the full table, which is in IRS Publication 590.

Although these tables are said to be "unisex," they are in fact female tables that are used for everyone. This results in a smaller required distribution for males. Technically, a unisex table would be an average of male and female. For example, if males had a life expectancy at 70 of 12 more years and females 16, then the average would be 14. When organizations calculate pensions based on life expectancies, they use the actual percentage of males and females and determine a weighted average. However, the IRS simply uses the female life expectancies throughout their tables.

Table 9.4 is primarily for people who inherit an IRA. Chapter 16 shows how to calculate the distribution, but Table 9.4 shows the single life expectancy tables as early as age 5.

The Future

We are living longer and healthier than at any time in human history. Today's advanced medicines and surgical techniques are ever pushing the age envelope. We are learning how to keep our arteries clear and our hearts strong. The near future could be the day of no wrinkles, no white hair, and our brains ever learning and remembering. An age of unheard of and never imagined quality of life.

This future is phenomenal and the facts fascinating. Could we control and end Alzheimer's, arthritis, cancer, dementia, heart disease, and strokes? We are slowly bending the will of nature with the prospect of future generations being able to dream that they could live forever.

What then of our lives? What would a career length be? and what of retirement? We could work to age 100 or 120, and then still settle down to a long retirement. Leaving work at age 65 with 85 years of retirement would seem

TABLE 9.4 IRA—Single—Life Expectancy Table

AGE		AGE		AGE		AGE		AGE	
5	76.6	30	52.2	55	28.6	80	9.5	105	1.8
6	75.6	31	51.2	56	27.7	81	8.9	106	1.6
7	74.7	32	50.2	57	26.8	82	8.4	107	1.4
8	73.7	33	49.3	58	25.9	83	7.9	108	1.3
9	72.7	34	48.3	59	25.0	84	7.4	109	1.1
10	71.7	35	47.3	60	24.2	85	6.9	110	1.0
11	70.7	36	46.4	61	23.3	86	6.5	111	0.9
12	69.7	37	45.4	62	22.5	87	6.1	112	0.8
13	68.8	38	44.4	63	21.6	88	5.7	113	0.7
14	67.8	39	43.5	64	20.8	89	5.3	114	0.6
15	66.8	40	42.5	65	20.0	90	5.0	115 and older	0.5
16	65.8	41	41.5	66	19.2	91	4.7		
17	64.8	42	40.6	67	18.4	92	4.4		
18	63.9	43	39.6	68	17.6	93	4.1		
19	62.9	44	38.7	69	16.8	94	3.9		
20	61.9	45	37.7	70	16.0	95	3.7		
21	60.9	46	36.8	71	15.3	96	3.4		
22	59.9	47	35.9	72	14.6	97	3.2		
23	59.0	48	34.9	73	13.9	98	3.0		
24	58.0	49	34.0	74	13.2	99	2.8		
25	57.0	50	33.1	75	12.5	100	2.7		
26	56.0	51	32.2	76	11.9	101	2.5		
27	55.1	52	31.3	77	11.2	102	2.3		
28	54.1	53	30.4	78	10.6	103	2.1		
29	53.1	54	29.5	79	10.0	104	1.9		

Source: IRS Publication 590 and Table V of the IRS Publication 939.

ludicrous. Would we even want to retire? Would retirement have any meaning at all?

In Shakespeare's Seven Ages of Man speech in *As You Like It,* he characterized us in our last stage appropriately in physical terms. In his day that pertained to people in their 50s and earlier. Even today, however, his words ring true as people enter their late 80s and early 90s:

> . . . Last scene of all, that ends this strange eventful history, is second childishness and mere oblivion; sans teeth, sans eyes, sans taste, sans everything.

The sciences of medicine and chemistry could push this demise twice as long as when the Bard wrote his words, although, for the foreseeable future, there will probably still be oblivion whenever we reach the end:

> We work and play one hundred years
> Clear mind and frame we do careers,
> Retire strong for twenty more
> It lasts a century and a score.
>
> Then finally rest our altered bones
> As science cease, our body moans,
> We suddenly quit and come apart
> And from this life we now depart.

CHAPTER 10

Discriminate against the Older Person at Your Own Peril

Memo to GenX manager: When you treat an older worker with disrespect, consider that 20 years hence some GenZ manager may do the same to you. When you don't give challenging assignments to older workers, can you then blithely dismiss them as not on the cutting edge? You, in fact, have an opportunity to transform the potential of older age, so when you arrive there you will have enhanced your own long-term self-respect.

Our country has struggled with racial, ethnic, and gender discrimination, and more recently disability discrimination. There is one more to add to that list: discrimination toward the older person. The term ageism was coined in 1969 by Robert Butler in his book *Why Survive: Being Old in America* (Harper & Row: New York). Since then there has been a slow but steady progress.

In fact, most older people don't want to play the stereotyped role of the "older person." This role is assigned differently in different societies, but often in ours, it refers to those who are physically and mentally weak, slow in step, rigid in mind, and, all too frequently, useless.

This was not always so. No one worried that George Washington was too old at 56 to be president. He finished his second term when he was 64. As late as the turn of the century, 1900, an older person was generally in control of the household and respected. On the farm, older people were the font of knowledge about weather and planting. In other countries, the elderly have been given special consideration as well. Japan, for example, has long been known to venerate the old.

But the more we became an industrialized country, the less we venerated older people. They couldn't keep up with younger workers on the assembly line. The Depression even called for the older worker to step aside so younger workers could get jobs. We slowly evolved into the concept that the young should rule the day.

The Role of the New Old

But work today is less factory and more white collar where knowledge counts. Many older people are keeping in shape, learning academics, and enjoying sex. In hundreds of ways, older people are no longer accepting the limiting role of old age that they were taught. They don't want to play the "old" game anymore.

The new role is a multivaried nonrole, if you will. Older people are doing their own thing, according to their individual curiosities and predilections. The older person is even working and thriving. The monolithic stereotype of the old is breaking down into individual differences, just like any other age.

What is old? The "old" like the concept of "middle age" is a subjective one, besides a cultural one. It doesn't seem that long ago that age 65 meant that you were old. Today, we think of age 85 and later as being old age.

Hope in Medical Advances

There are almost 100,000 people over age 100 today. In a couple of decades there could be over 1 million. As science continues its onslaught on Alzheimer's, coronary disease, and a host of older afflictions, more of us will join the very old. Such revelations as DNA research and stem cells that can rebuild our aging bodies, portend a future of an extended, healthy aging life.

It will continue to shape the concept society has of the older person, and even of ourselves once there. A nonmedical reason this progress will probably continue is what Bill Arnone, a friend and colleague indicates, "Older people have not only money and life experience, but most importantly they have, as a group, a positive attitude."

A negative concept of an older worker deprives our society of the full use of older people. It relegates them to family and leisure, which is fine for many, but not for all. It prevents older people from having the freedom to pursue jobs, if they wish. Thus, it ultimately prevents some older workers from having the freedom to pursue personally fulfilling opportunities.

A Final Word

Some older people want to work, some need to work. So, young manager, reap what you will sow. Like other pivotal aspects of life, the stones we throw could come back to fall on ourselves. Barring untimely death, we all become old.

CHAPTER 11

The Why of Retirement: How Each Generation Creates Its Own Retirement

Below the tapestry of our everyday lives, generational roots have a surprising pull on us. They often even dictates our money habits. The concept of generations explains why your parents or grandparents still save everything in their attic, retaining the frugality from the Depression many distant years ago.

Usually we think of generations in terms of specific music, dress, and pop culture—a younger generation responding to a desire to be different. In the 1960s, long hair in men and the braless look for women overwhelmed the Depression-World War II stodgies. Today, it's tattoos, pierced noses and bellies, and more. One generation's young challenges the last. That's when you hear, "What's happening to young kids today?"

But generations also explain something deeper—the embedded patterns of behavior and thought that are part of a common experience for each 18-year slice of the American time line. The Depression and World War II gave an imprint to that generation as does the technology revolution to the present one.

Which Generation Are You From?

World War I	Born 1890 to 1908
Depression-War	Born 1909 to 1927
Balance	Born 1928 to 1945
Baby Boom	Born 1946 to 1964
Generation X	Born 1965 to 1983
Generation Y	Born 1984 to 2002

Actually, generations are cultural demarcations of secular trends within an 18-year cohort of common experiences such as the rise of the independence and entrepreneurship of the individual, the loosening of the bonds of family, and inclusion of all ethnic and racial peoples in our society. These are all secular trends that give a snapshot to a generation. And so too, generations make their mark with an evolving idea of retirement.

Because retirement started in 1940, it caught the World War I crowd off guard and was a pleasant surprise. The Depression-War generation was the first to be able to take advantage of it. The Balance group was the first to be able to plan for it and by being confident enough to change jobs, began to diversify it. The Baby Boomers covet it and are planning to extend it to include entrepreneurship as part of retirement itself. The GenXers appear to see a distant retirement in more realistic terms, think Social Security will not be there for them and, in general, are not sure what awaits them.

World War I Generation: Disillusionment (1890 to 1908)

This generation suffered through the Great War to end all wars, 1914 to 1918. The war was the overwhelming event that shaped people's lives at that time. What troubled them most was how it could have happened in the first place. Wars were assumed to be part of the past. After the last bullet was finally fired, historians, psychologists, and writers searched for answers in a great outpouring of articles and books. *All Quiet on the Western Front,* for example, was a poignant exploration of war itself.

Many people felt disillusioned. The avant-garde of the generation wound their way to Paris and were dubbed the Lost Generation. World War I led people, as I saw them in their 80s and 90s, to be very realistic and somewhat cynical about money.

Depression-War Generation: The Beginning of Retirement (1909 to 1927)

This generation's lot in life was to endure two tragedies: the worst economic disaster in modern times—the Depression of the 1930s, followed immediately by World War II. Seeing hunger firsthand and people's savings snatched away by an out-of-control economy etched frugality and uncertainty indelibly in their brains. World War II, an overpowering and unsettling experience, added to the insecurity of this generation. In counseling these Depression-War retirees, I can see these powerful experiences still influencing many of their financial decisions. Work, any work, for the Depression-War cohort was the primary objective.

My 80-something friend, Richard Bobbe, now retired and active in many community and personal endeavors, sums up his generation, "We worked since school, when we could. There was no sense of planning our finances. We were simply struggling to get by. As a generation, we had to be careful about money and didn't realize that these habits and attitudes would pay off for us over the long haul." And, here Richard's face lights up, "We never thought about retirement, never had a perception of it as so many people seem to have today. And how did we end up financially? Fortunately, quite comfortably."

Before World War II, pensions were paid mainly to veterans (who received them for war-related disabilities) and to some police officers and firefighters for length of service. According to the 1994 research book the *Columbia Retirement Handbook,* there were only about 11,000 workers in 1929 receiving pensions from private companies.

However, having survived the Depression and the war, returning servicemen were glad to dedicate themselves to a company, any company, and companies reciprocated by offering benefits including pensions for workers' long-term financial security. Security is a human fundamental need, but was never felt more strongly than by this generation.

With Social Security in place, companies offering pensions for lifetime employment, and a saving mentality established, the Depression-War generation was the first to cobble together what we now assume to be a right—retirement. It is ironic that people of this generation, who started out so insecurely with respect to money, are living the ultimate financial fantasy: 30 years of work followed by 30 years of a leisurely retirement.

Balance Generation: Responsibility and Opportunity (1928 to 1945)

This generation requires some explanation because it is little understood. Most people assume, even when pressed to think about it, that the Baby Boomers come immediately after the Depression-War generation, yet there is an 18-year gap between the two, which is the average length of a generation. It is filled by a generation aptly labeled the Balance generation, because it was shaped primarily by two very different, and balancing, forces—a sense of responsibility and a sense of opportunity.

The experience of their parents, who lived through the Depression as children or young adults, forced a sense of seriousness about life onto their balance generation children. Life could be difficult and was to be met by hard work. The Balancers were not old enough to have served in World War II and experience those horrors firsthand. Conversely, the Balance generation experienced great opportunities, first by being able to go to college in large numbers and then by having unrivaled career opportunities during the roaring postwar economy. It gave this generation a sense of confidence that showed in many of the things they have accomplished, including considerable job-hopping in contrast to the preceding generation.

It has sometimes been dubbed the silent generation, which it surely is not. Hip-rocking Elvis Presley (born in 1935) and piano-pounding Jerry Lee Lewis (1935), along with all the other early rockers, can hardly be called silent. They burst on the scene with bravado and verve, singing "You Ain't Nothin' but a Hound Dog," and "Great Balls of Fire." The Beatles added to the cacophony with the fab four of John, Paul, George, and Ringo, all born between 1940 and 1943. This generation changed the course of music and a lot of other things in our culture.

Voices from this generation were heard on many fronts. The civil rights leader Martin Luther King, Jr. (1929), feminist Gloria Steinem (1934), and consumer activist Ralph Nader (1934), were all of this generation, as were such radicals as the 1960s' Abbie Hoffman (1936) and Jerry Rubin (1938). So were

Time's 1995 Man of the Year, Newt Gingrich (1943), along with Mikhail Gorbachev (1931), Vaclav Havel (1936), and Lech Walesa (1943).

With respect to careers, this generation was the first to break the work contract, as early as the mid- to late-1960s. Opportunities were so prevalent that they simply moved from one company to another if their talents were not appreciated or if other companies wooed them away. Because they were not burdened with the insecurity or dutifulness of their parents, they had few reservations about changing jobs. They also were in demand because they worked with a strong sense of purpose and accomplishment.

How does this generation see pensions? Since they were the ones to move from company to company, they have less of an expectation for or a sense of entitlement to them. This generation, with its sense of opportunity, sees pensions as one of several ways to retirement, along with 401(k) plans, Social Security, personal savings, and yes, work.

The people I'm counseling into retirement now are primarily from this generation, and I can see these balancing forces still at play. Retirement, like work, is not seen in a monolithic way as it was for the Depression-War people. Retirement is more than a leisurely life; it is a time to balance a variety of activities, including continuing or new employment. The Bureau of Labor Statistics has even documented this work activity. Since the first Balancers reached 65, in 1993, the percentage of people working over the age of 65 has started to increase. This is an inflection point, braking a continual downward trend from the 1950s.

Baby Boom Generation: Great Expectations (1946 to 1964)

Born in great numbers just after World War II, this generation came into a world full of optimism. The Depression was already a distant memory and World War II had faded away by the time they reached their impressionistic age. We were on top of the world economically. Landon Jones, former Managing Editor of *People* magazine, wrote the definitive book on this generation in his 1980 book, aptly titled, *Great Expectations: America and the Baby Boom Generation* (Coward, McCann, & Geoghegan: New York).

At times, this generation can seem to take things for granted. In 1987, while I was giving a retirement speech to a management group, a younger person in the audience rose to make a striking statement befitting the "take it for granted attitude" of his generation. He said that as a baby boomer he was not particularly worried about retirement because his father was about to retire with some comfort. He, as a younger person, was better educated and better prepared for the sophisticated and challenging world today, and ergo, he was easily going to retire.

I remember offering a caution. "Younger people are changing jobs frequently and thus not building up pensions. As world-class consumers, younger people are not accumulating retirement savings. And many young people say Social Security will not be there for them." And then the bottom-line question: "Just how will you retire with no money?" I remember that he and the audience were at a loss for words. Perhaps what was so easily assumed may not be so.

Since it is natural for this generation to have high expectations, it is somewhat disconcerting for Boomers to realize that retirement for some may actually be difficult to attain. In truth, this generation will experience great variation in retirement. Some will still retire with ease; others will find it delayed to as late as age 70 or 75; and some will not have enough funds to retire at all. In fact, one of my several motivations in writing this book is to help Boomers set in motion a purposeful plan for their individual retirement.

With the leading edge of this generation now in their mid-50s and beginning to plan seriously for retirement, the subject of pensions has now flashed across the radar screen. However, pensions have held little meaning. The 401(k) plans are ideal because you are in control. You can see your plan balances daily, if desired, and you decide how your money is invested. If you change jobs, the money goes with you.

To the extent that retirement may be difficult, self-employment and alternative careers offer the Boomers a way to continue to earn money on their own terms. They'll be in control. Being your own boss is the ultimate fantasy job. Alternative careers are those you deliberately choose after finally discovering who you are.

Generation X: A Sense of Reality (1965 to 1983)

This generation sees the potential of the good life, but realizes they'll have to earn it. They already have a sense of their future, and they want to start planning early, very early, like now. It's a generation that I had expected to deal with some time in the future, but they have already made appointments.

Named by Douglas Coupland in his book *Generation X: Tales for an Accelerated Culture* (1991, St. Martin's Press: New York), this group has been interpreted as a "slacker generation," which it is not. Coupland writes about those who withdrew from the merry-go-round of status and money to seek more meaning in their personal lives. Perhaps they will embrace some form of this noble notion as their own generational concept of retirement. They also seem to want to accumulate less material stuff than boomers, but that may be more a function of not yet getting to midlife where accumulation seems more prevalent.

Whatever idea of retirement this generation evolves to, pensions are not even on their screens. The 401(k) plan is all they know and it allows them to plan their future. Traditional pensions by their nature are complicated and difficult if not impossible to project. Just try to get your company to tell you what your pension will be 30 years in the future. At least GenXers can project their 401(k) balances with a simple computer calculator.

Generation Y (1984 to 2002)

This generation now ranges from the maternity ward to high school. It's a generation that has had a compressed childhood, having been bombarded with pop culture that focuses on younger and younger kids.

Although too early to tell how it will deal with their circumstances, it is certain to be a generation that feels comfortable with new communication technology, wireless Internet for instance, and will probably be comfortable with technology all around them: at work, at home, and wherever they recreate.

Summary

So, what is a generation? Basically it's a state of mind for each life segment of age cohorts, resulting in differences from music to social ideas. For retirement, these differences are reflected in people's plans and actions with respect to their finances and how they define the activity we call retirement. Observing these differences has given me an additional tool to provide more effective planning for my clients.

The Depression-War generation strove for security, and they were able to create the first, if monolithic, concept of retirement—100 percent work and then 100 percent retirement. They reached a financial level of comfort the Depression had given them little hope for. In a phrase, the Depression-War generation has given us:

Hard work has its rewards.

The Balancers next created a more diverse concept combining work, leisure, and family. Their sense of work was enhanced by their early experiences of getting a warm and fuzzy feeling from companies. You knew that if you worked hard, and smart, you would get increasingly responsible jobs. You had security from your competence. Thus, the Balancers have given us a sense of balance in our lives and a perspective of work:

Work is not all bad (and leisure not all good).

The Boomers with their high expectations force the idea of getting what you want, controlling one's destiny. The ME generation wants it now and on their terms. The energy, independence, and desire for control will translate into a retirement of:

Starting businesses and alternative careers.

Generation Xers seem to have a more realistic view, perhaps to fit a more realistic world. Retirement may come or not, but a focus on a more meaningful life not only can shape their lives, but can provide their children a better life, beyond materialistic terms. Thus, GenXers can see the future as:

Personal meaning to provide a greater quality of life.

Can We Predict the Future?

Can a projection of generations give us a clue to the future of retirement? Not by unknown events yet to be thrust on generations to come, but perhaps by extending secular trends that are evolving and will probably continue to develop.

Here is a guess. Retirement will continue to be a more diverse event, more individually idiosyncratic. Some will retire on time, but many may be forced to delay it. Some may not be able to muster the financial resources to retire at all. For those for whom it will be less attainable, it may force a refocusing on their careers, and even force a change into a whole new career late in life. Finally, as people live longer, people may go in and then back out of retirement to replenish their financial resources.

Above all, I can predict that retirement will remain a hotly desired goal for almost everyone.

CHAPTER 12

Retirement on a Shoestring

This could be your most important chapter. If you cringe when you read an article that proclaims that you will need a million plus to retire and have no way to get there, you may find a measure of comfort here.

Ned and Sally

Ned and Sally only have a total of $126,000 between the bank and mutual funds, plus two small pensions and Social Security. They are enjoying retirement, especially time with their five grandchildren.

How do they do it? They have a standard of living that's appropriate for their financial resources—their income determines their expenses. Their planning starts with how much income they have, which then defines what they can afford. Their expenses fit into their income.

I can assure you that Ned and Sally do enjoy their lifestyle. They enjoy the simple pleasures of being close to and active with their family. They often babysit their grandchildren, a double pleasure of being with them and knowing they are helping their kids who have busy careers. They eat out twice a week, once at the local steak house and once at the diner on Highway 45. "What more would you want out of life?" they ask me.

Their pensions of $8,100, Social Security of $16,410, and interest of $6,300 (total $30,810), even allow them to save about $1,800 a year. Their house is paid for, and their real estate taxes are only $2,700. They pay no federal nor state income taxes. Furthermore, their medical plan is a good one, and they spend very little out-of-pocket for doctors' visits and pharmaceuticals.

My colleague Robin Sherwood tells of a person who approached her and asked, "I'm going to have an income in retirement of about $35,000, is that enough?" After a moment of contemplation, she countered with the right amount of generality: "If you shop at Saks Fifth Avenue probably not, if at Kmart maybe."

It is a balancing act after all. You want your resources (income and assets) to be enough to equal your lifestyle (your expenses).

Jerry

Unlike Ned and Sally, Jerry has investment assets but neither pensions nor other income sources. He lives off his investments of $500,000, which generate income of about $40,000 a year. He never stayed long enough at any one organization to have a pension and he's too early for Social Security. His eastern metropolitan city apartment is rent controlled at $830 a month. He is just age 56 and does not plan to dip into his investment principal until sometime after 60. He has a network of friends and spends most of his time in libraries studying history, his longtime love. His one luxury is bicycling which often finds him on country roads. "I don't have to work anymore, so why should I?"

Backward Planning

Retiring on a shoestring is backward retirement planning. You first determine what you can afford and then back your retirement plan into that reality.

But a modest retirement can be a good retirement. Many people today live a rewarding and satisfying retirement at bargain basement levels. It is a matter of finding whatever combination of income and assets you can muster to provide the lifestyle that it permits. Is that enough for you? That will be the question with which you must wrestle.

How to Cut Back on Expenses

Is a simplified, less expensive lifestyle possible today? For some, making judicious reductions in expenses allow for a retirement. It's not for everyone, or even for many, but for some it can offer an attractive lifestyle.

There are even some who want to abandon our expensive modern way of life and return to a more simple life, usually to a more rural setting. They reduce their expenses by growing some of their own food and making some of their own clothes, cutting up their credit cards, eschewing appliances like microwaves and toasters, and spending considerable time reading and discussing the ideas of the day with friends and neighbors.

How to Increase Income

Seasonal jobs could be the ticket, like wrapping gifts at a department store or being Santa at the local mall. Possible summertime jobs are scooping ice cream or working at a local tourist spot.

Alternative careers can provide self-fulfillment besides bringing in more income: One person always wanted to be a cook at a bed and breakfast. Another wanted to cane chairs and other furniture. Another wanted to travel and write articles about it. Another wanted to teach at the local college. Another always wanted to start a business, any business, and so forth (see Figure 12.1).

The next step is to complete the expense worksheet at the end of Chapter 7. This will tell you how close your retirement expenses will be to your expected retirement income.

Living Overseas

There are places where American retirement communities thrive, like Mexico or Costa Rica, among others. They can be the lowest of low-cost living arrangements with cheap household and yard help. It's estimated that over 2 million Americans are doing so. My good friend Leland Kenower who is considering living overseas for a couple of months each year when he retires says, "I can live a tropical lifestyle that I used to see in the movies."

RETIREMENT INCOME

Pensions	$_____
Social Security	_____
Investment income	_____
Other income (part-time work, rentals, etc.)	_____
Total Income	$_____

FIGURE 12.1 A Simple Worksheet.

The Secret

Whereas most who plan retirement start from the proposition that they should wait until their retirement income will be sufficient to afford their lifestyle, for some, it's the other way around. They know what their income is, or will be, and adjust their expenses and plans accordingly. It doesn't seem like much of a trick to those who do it. It's common sense. And that's how people retire on a shoestring.

Step 3. At the Cusp of Retirement—Time for the "I'm about to Retire Worksheet"

Retirement is finally here. Perhaps it's six months or even a year away, but importantly it's close enough that you can actually taste it. You've set the date, if not with your employer at least in your mind. No more speculation. Now you have real numbers with a real date.

To detail your plan, you'll need your organization to give you specific pension amounts, if any. You know the amount of money in your 401(k), 403(b), 457, Keogh, or IRA accounts. You will have contacted Social Security and know what you will be receiving as a benefit, either immediately, or if you're too young, what your benefit will be at 62 or older when you start to collect it. You also may have plans to work part-time and know how much you might expect. Now you need to put your numbers down on paper and see how it all works out as a sound retirement plan.

You're ready for the "I'm about to Retire Worksheet" (Figure 13.1 on page 126).

The example of Tom and Marie, who are about to retire, can help you understand the worksheet. Tom is 64 and has been self-employed in the advertising field. Marie is 63 and has worked for a major corporation in their general counsel's office. Two tables are associated with the worksheet: Table 13.1, to project inflation, and Table 13.2, to estimate income taxes.

	AT RETIREMENT	5 YEARS LATER	10 YEARS LATER
RETIREMENT INCOME			
Pensions	————	————	————
Social Security (see Table 13.1 for 5- and 10-year projections)	————	————	————
Other income (part-time work, rentals, trusts, etc.)	————	————	————
Total Investments	————	————	————
Investment income	————	————	————
Income before taxes (add all income)	————	————	————
Taxes (see Table 13.2)	————	————	————
Income after taxes	————	————	————
Total Income	════	════	════
RETIREMENT EXPENSES			
Estimated retirement expenses (see Table 13.1 for 5- and 10-year projections)	————	————	————
Expenses to increase/decrease (vacations, mortgage, etc.)	————	————	————
Total Expenses	════	════	════
EXCESS/SHORTFALL	════	════	════

FIGURE 13.1 I'm about to Retire Worksheet.

After looking at their retirement numbers and some of their thinking, we review additional pointers that may be important for you as you complete the worksheet for yourself.

Finally, we cover some other important retirement issues, such as medical insurance and how to get additional income in retirement if needed.

Example

Figure 13.2 on page 128 shows how Tom and Marie completed the worksheet.

Example Explanation

First, Tom and Marie received information from their organizations that they would receive $26,300 in pensions. They each selected the 50 percent joint and

EXAMPLE 127

TABLE 13.1 Inflation

INFLATION RATE	YEARS			
	1	2	3	4
1%	1.01	1.02	1.03	1.04
2%	1.02	1.04	1.06	1.08
3%	1.03	1.06	1.09	1.13
4%	1.04	1.08	1.12	1.17
5%	1.05	1.10	1.16	1.22
6%	1.06	1.12	1.19	1.26
INFLATION RATE	5	10	15	20
1%	1.05	1.10	1.16	1.22
2%	1.10	1.22	1.35	1.49
3%	1.16	1.34	1.56	1.81
4%	1.22	1.48	1.80	2.19
5%	1.28	1.63	2.08	2.65
6%	1.34	1.79	2.40	3.21

Note: Figures rounded to two decimal points.

survivor pension option. Since the pensions are not inflation protected, they also put $26,300 in the columns for 5 and 10 years.

Second, they determined that they would each receive Social Security benefits—$11,900 for Tom and $12,200 for Marie—for a total of $24,100. Since Social Security payments increase by inflation, they used Table 13.1 to determine what the benefit could be 5 and 10 years hence. They decided to use an inflation projection of 3 percent, using factors of 1.16 and 1.34 from the table. This

TABLE 13.2 Estimated Tax

If total income is:	TAX PERCENTAGE
$20,000–$30,000	10
$30,000–$50,000	15
$50,000–$100,000	25
over $100,000	30

	AT RETIREMENT	5 YEARS LATER	10 YEARS LATER
RETIREMENT INCOME			
Pensions	$ 26,300	$26,300	$ 26,300
Social Security (see Table 13.1 for 5- and 10-year projections)	24,100	27,956	32,294
Other income (part-time work, rentals, trusts, etc.)	15,000	————	————
Total Investments $750,000			
Investment Income	37,500	37,500	37,500
Income before taxes (add all income)	102,900	91,756	96,094
Taxes (see Table 13.2)	30,870	22,939	24,024
Income after taxes	72,030	68,817	72,070
RETIREMENT EXPENSES			
Estimated retirement expenses (see Table 13.1 for 5- and 10-year projections)	60,000	69,600	80,400
Expenses to increase/decrease (vacations, mortgage, etc.)	————	(5,500)	(5,500)
Total Expenses	60,000	64,100	74,900
EXCESS/SHORTFALL	12,030	4,717	(2,830)

FIGURE 13.2   I'm about to Retire Worksheet for Tom and Marie.

results in 5- and 10-year projected benefits of $27,956 and $32,294 ($24,100 times 1.16 equals $27,500 and $24,100 times 1.34 equals $32,294). If you review Table 7.1 in Chapter 7, it may help you select an inflation average you would like to use.

Third, Tom estimated that he would do part-time work for about three years at about $15,000 each year. Thus, there would be an additional $15,000 income initially that would not be there in 5 and 10 years.

Fourth, they estimated the income from their investments. Their total investments are about $750,000, counting their 401(k)s, IRAs, and other investments. They assumed that they could safely take about 5 percent each year from the investments, as a combination of income and expected appreciation,

EXAMPLE 129

resulting in an income of about $37,500 each year ($750,000 times 0.05 or 5 percent, equals $37,500).

Fifth, and finally, they determined what their income taxes could be. Using Table 13.2, they used the percentage of 30 percent for years with income over $100,000 and 25 percent when under. This resulted in estimated taxes of $30,870, $22,939, and $24,024 ($102,900 times 0.3 or 30 percent, equals $30,870, $91,756 times 0.25 or 25 percent, equals $22,939, and $96,094 times 0.25 or 25 percent, equals $24,024). These taxes were then subtracted from the gross incomes for the net of $72,030, $68,817, and $72,070.

Then, Tom and Marie turned to their estimated expenses. After considerable review, they estimated that their expenses will be $60,000 as they begin retirement. They used the form shown in Figure 7.2 to list their expenses.

To project what those expenses would be as their retirement years roll on, they decided to use 3 percent, and found the factors of 1.16 and 1.34 for 5 and 10 years respectively from Table 13.1. This would mean their expenses in 5 and 10 years would be $69,600 and $80,400 ($60,000 times 1.16 equals $69,600 and $60,000 times 1.34 equals $80,400).

They also know that their mortgage would be paid off in 4 years, and thus they subtracted the mortgage payments of $5,500 from expenses in 5 and 10 years. This resulted in their final expense figures: $60,000 as they start retirement, $64,100 in 5 years, and $74,900 in 10 years.

Finally, Tom and Marie needed to compare their income and expenses. Their income exceeded their expenses for the first year of retirement by $12,030, so they felt comfortable financially. However, in 5 years that cushion would drop to $4,717, and in 10 the estimate shows a shortfall of $2,830. Inflation would be eroding their initial financial comfort.

They would be watching their investments as closely as their expenses and were hopeful that, in 10 years, they could dip slightly into their investment principal to make up the difference. They reasoned that taking out about $3,000 from their investments would be less than one-half of 1 percent ($3,000 divided by $750,000 equals 0.004, or 0.4 percent). They would monitor their expenses and investments each year, again making 5- and 10-year projections. Chapter 15 focuses on this subject.

Selected Worksheet Items

The *interval* you use for the worksheet doesn't have to be 5 and 10 years for the second and third column. For you, maybe a 3-year interval would be appropriate, or even a 1-year interval. A 1-year interval is recommended if you are unsure of your income or expenses or expect significant changes for the first several years. Further, it is not recommended that you stop using the worksheet once these three milestones in time are over. Redo the worksheet whenever you want to or need to monitor your retirement situation throughout your retirement.

For *pension amount,* you may have to consider the options available in your plan, if any. Chapter 14 provides a discussion of these options. That's where the 50 percent joint and survivor pension option among others is reviewed.

As you use Table 13.1, you might want to turn to Chapter 2 where the subject of present and future value is reviewed. Most people don't have a lot of experience projecting values into the future and thus are not overly familiar with how to do so. Although you could use calculators (handheld or computer), that provide these projections, Table 13.1 provides the simplified method of factors. For example, if you wanted to project the value of your expenses just one year at 4 percent you first find the factor in the table. In this case it's 1.04. You then multiply the starting amount by this factor to get the result. Tom and Marie determined their first year's expenses to be $60,000. If they wanted to know what the expenses would be just after one year at a 4 percent increase, they would first find the factor from Table 13.1, which is 1.04. It would be calculated as $62,400 ($60,000 times 1.04 equals $62,400). The table rounds the factors to two decimal places, which for mathematicians may be disconcerting, but for everyone else is easier to use.

What if your *expenses exceed your income?* This is a critical and difficult aspect of retirement planning. In our example, this occurred for Tom and Marie in their 10th year. They would have to decrease expenses or take some of the principal from investments, or a little of both. If you take from principal, however, you would want to deplete the principal slowly so it would last a long time, based on your projected life expectancy. To help in this calculation, Chapter 15 has three tables that do just that (Tables 15.2 to 15.4).

Say, you had $100,000 and wanted to know how long it would last if you took out 8 percent each year. Assume that the investment would continue to earn 8 percent, and that the amount taken out would increase each year by 3 percent to account for inflation. The answer, using Table 15.3, is 20 years. Each of the three tables presents the same information from a different viewpoint.

For *income taxes* in retirement, you may have some pleasant surprises. First, there are no FICA, or Social Security taxes, unless you continue to work. This is essentially 7.65 percent of your working salary and for the self-employed,

15.3 percent. It's capped in 2001 at $80,400; however, it continues at 1.45 percent for Medicare A. Second, Social Security benefits could even be tax free, if your income for this purpose is under $25,000 if single, or $32,000 if married. Check Chapter 8 for the details. There is also a higher standard deduction once you reach age 65. All of these can make income taxes far more palatable in retirement.

Insurance Issues

Your *medical insurance coverage* is perhaps the most critical financial issue besides the direct income of pensions and investments. It is most important to have sufficient coverage for doctors, hospitalization, and prescription drugs. Once you turn 65, then Medicare A and B become your primary medical insurance, but you usually need a medigap supplement. Either your employer would provide this extra coverage or you may need to purchase it on your own.

If you don't have medical coverage when you leave an employer, you may be eligible for COBRA, which allows you to extend your current medical benefits for up to 18 months. COBRA is an acronym for the 1985 legislation that created this right, the Consolidated Omnibus Budget Reconciliation Act. You'll have to pay your employer's rate, or slightly higher, but COBRA guarantees that you can be covered.

If you're *over 65 and still working*, make sure you sign up with Medicare, Part A, which doesn't cost you a monthly premium. You don't have to sign up for Part B, which costs $50 a month in 2001. If you're still working and your employer has medical coverage for you, then there is usually no reason to have Medicare Part B, because your employer's plan is primary and Medicare Part B would pay nothing. The government doesn't force you to pay for Part B if you

---

The 10 Medigap Supplement Plans

All 10 plans offer core benefits, but then each of the 10 plans, labeled A through J, offer more benefits. Plan A offers only the basic core benefits while Plan J is the most comprehensive, and most expensive. Plans H, I, and J offer increasing prescription drug plans. Plans C through J offer a foreign travel emergency plan. Since only these 10 plans can be sold, it is fairly easy to compare insurance company offerings.

would not use it. However, if you don't sign up for Medicare A at 65 in this case (to hold your place so to speak), then there would be an eventual 10 percent increase for Part B each year you didn't sign up for Medicare.

There is usually less of a need for *life insurance* once you have retired. As always, there should be a specific reason to have life insurance. Life insurance is critical when you're young and have a family. It can provide needed financial resources for the spouse and family if you die. In retirement, with the kids grown up and on their own, this life insurance need is often nonexistent. Life insurance can take on a role of providing liquidity to pay for estate taxes. However, with estate taxes supposedly being phased out, this life insurance need may be closing out (see Chapter 15).

There may be more of a need for *long-term care insurance* today. With Medicare providing almost no nursing home care, the costs could overwhelm your ability to pay for these expenses if necessary. The figures show that after age 85 there is a high likelihood that you will spend three years in a nursing home, or have similar care in your home. The average annual cost of care today can be $60,000 or more in urban areas.

Other Planning Issues

Where you *live* can impact your retirement expenses. The costs can vary depending on housing costs, real estate taxes, and income taxes. However, even states with income taxes often give tax breaks for seniors.

Establishing a specific *domicile* can avoid having two states trying to tax you when you have two potential residences. If you are a snowbird (with a summer and winter residence), you may want to establish one of the two locations as your official domicile. States do require you to be a resident of their state (and be taxed by them) if you in fact live in that state. What counts to qualify as a resident? Of course, a commonsense definition exists—if you only spend two weeks a year in a state you would hardly qualify. But when you truly spend a significant portion of the year in two states, then three major items usually establish your official domicile:

1. Where you have your regular checking and savings bank account

2. Where you vote

3. Where your car is registered

Having all three in a specific state often establishes your official residence for tax purposes.

If you expect an *inheritance,* it is difficult to know how to factor that into your finances. People are living longer than ever and with advances in medical care, an expected inheritance can be long in coming. Better to ignore, than to plan on it.

A little mentioned retirement phenomenon is called *paycheck withdrawal* and may afflict you. My colleague, Robin Sherwood, alerts retirees to this. She goes on to explain, "People are accustomed to getting a regular paycheck, but when retirement starts they are often left with an uneasy feeling at first because they have to create their own paycheck." It's a different mind-set and can cause financial disorientation in some until they get the hang of it. Those who receive a monthly pension and Social Security payments find this to be less of a problem. Those who have to live only on investment income and principal tend to have a harder time adjusting.

Finally, *work* could be part of your retirement. It could be just another boring job to earn extra money, or it could be an alternative career. It could be something you've always wanted to do like start a business, engage in a dream career you've wanted to pursue but never had time for, or something that just sounds like fun. One retired couple I know work only weekends, she in a gift shop and he at a hardware store. Not only does it give them some extra income for trips to national parks, but it gives them a needed sense of belonging and self-worth.

CHAPTER 14

The Technical Side of Retiring

It's what you know that counts. Burdensome rules are our modern-day Gordian knot. I mean, should you keep your 401(k) with your employer even though you're retired and only have limited withdrawal provisions; or should you switch to a Rollover IRA and have to decide anew how to invest money, avoiding, of course, the 20 percent withholding trap, not to mention how to deal with that loan you still have outstanding; or should you pay ordinary income tax on the trustee cost-basis of your employer stock and use net unrealized appreciation for the rest?

For over 20 years, as a retirement professional, I've helped people zigzag through this technical morass of the 15 percent excess tax (now, thankfully gone), 5- and 10-year averaging (of which 5-year is gone and 10-year is fading with time), the IRA age 70½ rules of recalculation versus term certain (finally simplified as of January 2001), net unrealized appreciation (still here), or the three methods of avoiding the IRA 10 percent penalty before age 59½ (still here). There are times that people come to me completely flummoxed, if not

Tax Highlight

As of 2001 New age 70½ minimum withdrawal rules for IRAs, 401(k)s, 403(b)s, 457s, and pensions. New table and simplified rules.

fuming, with this technical fandango. At times, even I am amazed at the inane complexity of it all. But it's a living.

There are at least two ongoing problems here. First, each year there are some changes in these rules. Of the 44,000 pages of the Tax Code, some sentences are erased and some are added. But, how to know which ones apply to you? The second problem is that people try to see logic in these rules. As Larry McCoombe, my longtime friend and colleague, has often said, "We can talk taxes and we can talk logic, but unfortunately not at the same time."

To assist you in finding the technical information you need, this chapter has been organized using the following four sections:

1. Decisions and distribution rules for pensions: traditional and cash balance plans.
2. Decisions and distribution rules for 401(k)s, 403(b)s, 457, SEP, SIMPLE, and Keogh plans.
3. Decisions and distribution rules for IRAs.
4. A game plan for your situation.

Decisions and Distribution Rules for Pensions: Traditional and Cash Balance Plans

Traditional Plans

If you have a traditional pension, meaning you receive a monthly payment when you retire, then the only decision you may have is what form of monthly payment you'll select, single-life, 50 percent joint and survivor, and so forth. Some pensions allow for a lump sum, as do almost all cash balance plans.

The single-life pension, or similarly named option, is usually selected if you are single. It provides the highest monthly payment from the pension plan and provides a payment for however long you live. It has no survivor payment. The single-life pension is calculated directly from whatever pension formula your organization has, usually factoring in your years of service and the final 3 or 5 years' average salary. For union workers, it may be a flat-benefit formula, which takes your years of service and multiplies it by a dollar number. All other pension options, 50 percent joint, or lump sum, are calculated from this single-life pension.

A 50 percent joint and survivor option is the most common pension option if you're married. It provides a reduced pension to pay for the potential survivor payment to your spouse. The reduction is often about 10 percent. For example, if your single-life pension was $1,000 a month, then selecting the 50 percent option would mean you receive about $900 a month. Then, if your spouse outlives you, he or she would receive 50 percent of the $900 for the rest of his or her life, or $450. If you selected a 100 percent joint and survivor option, then your pension would be reduced another approximate 10 percent, or to about $800, but your survivor would receive 100 percent of the $800. Some pension plans offer survivor percentages between 50 percent and 100 percent. You select the best option given other retirement resources you and your spouse have.

The law requires a spouse to waive her or his right to a survivor benefit if you wish to select a single-life or lump sum, should it be offered. The waiver must be in writing and within 90 days of retirement.

A lump-sum option is provided for by as many as 20 percent of organizations. This is a one-time, up-front payment instead of a monthly pension. But it is often a nettlesome decision. Consider a recent retiree, Victoria, who was given this lump-sum option by her company. Should she take the guaranteed annuity option that would safely pay her a lifetime benefit, or take the lump sum and try to invest it? It's more money at one time than she ever imagined to invest. Could she manage it well?

She went to investment firms and financial planners who either sold investments or charged a percentage based on her assets. All immediately recommended that she take the lump sum. She realized that it would be hard to get an unbiased opinion that would suit her situation.

After losing many hours of sleep over this decision, she decided to take the single-life annuity instead of the lump sum. Although the lump sum looked enticing, she decided that the long-term steadiness of the annuity suited her best and felt that investing the lump sum was too daunting a task.

For others, a lump sum could prove to be a better option. Typically, executives who have deferred compensation and stock option payments for the first several years of retirement may not need their pension payments for several years. A lump sum could be invested during this time and provide an eventually larger monthly payment. Also, if an individual intended to continue working at another firm and wanted the lump sum to grow until retirement a number of years down the road, then a lump sum could be the ideal option.

Often the decision to take a lump sum or not comes down to how comfortable you are with investing money. If you feel the money can be invested wisely, you may prefer the lump sum. If you feel uncomfortable with investing and want a guaranteed and steady income, you may lean toward the annuity.

A lump-sum pension can usually be rolled over into an IRA, and is the usual way to deal with it. However, the lump sum could have "nonqualified" money, meaning that not all of it can be rolled over. Your organization should tell you if your lump sum can be rolled over, and how much of it can. Once the lump sum is rolled over into an IRA, then the money must follow the rules for IRAs, which are detailed in this chapter under Decisions and Distribution Rules for IRAs.

If you were born before 1936, you have a one-time tax option to use 10-Year Averaging, which results in a lower tax than paying regular taxes on it. The averaging option can be best for a lump sum if you are going to spend it, perhaps to buy a condo or yacht.

If you roll the lump sum over into an IRA, then you pay ordinary income taxes on withdrawals, and a 10 percent early withdrawal penalty before age 59½. Also, as discussed later, at age 70½ you must take minimum withdrawals from IRAs.

A Social Security leveling option is sometimes offered and pays a larger benefit before you start Social Security. When you start Social Security, then

---

10-Year Averaging

RULES:

- Must have been born before 1936.
- For lump sums from pensions and 401(k)s.
- Must have been a plan participant for 5 years.
- Cannot use if you rolled over any pension or 401(k) plans in same calendar year.
- Form 4972 used with single 1986 tax rates.
- Special exclusion if lump sum is under $70,000.
- Also, special capital gain rate on amounts attributed to service before 1974.

EXAMPLE: 10-Year Averaging on $150,000 is $24,570.

the benefit is decreased. The intent of this option is to keep your total retirement income about the same as before and after you receive Social Security.

A term certain option is commonly offered but rarely used. Typically a 5- and 10-year term certain option pays a monthly amount for the rest of your life, but if you die before 5 or 10 years are up, then the remaining payments would be paid to a named beneficiary or your estate. Say you selected a 5-year certain benefit and died after only 2 years into retirement, then the remaining 3 years would be paid out. You might consider this option if you had a minor in your care, and you wanted to protect that person for a specific period of time.

Cash Balance Plans

This is the newer version of your Dad's pension. There is always a specific "balance" which can be rolled over into an IRA, not only at retirement, but anytime you leave your firm. Thus, younger employees are comfortable with this type of plan. They know how much is in the plan each year and that it is portable if they leave.

Your plan balance can almost always be rolled over into an IRA, but you will need to check with your organization to determine if all of it can be rolled over.

How to Select the Best Option

There are several considerations when you are confronted with pension options. First, if you're single, there is usually little decision, simply take the highest amount. If however, you have the care of a minor or disabled child, you may wish to consider another option to protect that individual. Second, if you're married, then you need to lay out the various retirement sources of income and decide the best pension option given the various sources of income for you and your spouse. For example, if both spouses work and can receive about the same amounts of pensions, they might appropriately take their single-life option. This would give them the highest amounts while they were both alive, as well as when only one survives.

Monthly pensions are taxed as regular income, except to the extent that you contributed to it. Many organizations contribute the full amount to the pension, and thus, the pension is fully taxable to you. If, however, you have contributed to your pension, your organization will tell you each year how much is taxable through a 1099 tax summary form.

Many states have a set annual exclusion for pensions and IRA payments. It may not be as much as your pension, but it offers some welcome tax relief.

Decisions and Distribution Rules for 401(k)s, 403(b)s, 457, SEP, SIMPLE, and Keogh Plans

Most often, 401(k)s and Keoghs are paid only as lump sums, whereas 403(b)s and 457s are commonly paid in annuity forms. SEPs and SIMPLEs are already IRAs and thus follow the IRA rules.

The 401(k) plans are the accumulation of your, as well as your employer's, contributions and investments. They are almost always paid as lump sums, although a few plans offer annuity or installment payments.

The lump sum can be rolled over into an IRA. Your 401(k) plan could be an amalgam of a previous savings plan and the newer before-tax contribution feature. Also, some plans allow for current after-tax contributions. After-tax amounts beginning in 2002 can be rolled over, or given back to you tax free.

More and more employers are allowing you the option of keeping your money in the plan, even though you are retired. They even will let you keep it in after age 70½ when typically plans had forced the money out. There was a realization, especially by the investment providers of 401(k) plans that, if the money could stay in the plan, they would still receive the management fee for that money. In truth, some employees wanted this option as well.

If you are single and have a sizable plan balance, you may want to think twice about leaving your money with your 401(k) plan at retirement. Heirs cannot roll their eventual distribution into an IRA—only a spouse has that right. Thus, say, a person who has a million dollars in the plan, dies; then the heir(s) must take the money out by the end of the year following death and pay ordinary income on the whole amount. If the money had been rolled over into an IRA, then the heir(s) would have the option to take only portions of the IRA each year and only have to pay tax on that portion. Chapter 16 explains this further.

When and if you do take your lump sum and roll it over into an IRA, use the *direct rollover* method. It prevents an automatic 20 percent tax withholding that employers are mandated to apply. Your employer will provide information on this method and the forms to do so.

If you were born before 1936 and you do take your lump sum and want to pay taxes on it, you might be eligible to use 10-Year Averaging, as noted earlier.

You may have employer stock in your 401(k) plan. Companies often make their contributions in their own stock. Come time for distribution, however, this company stock can receive special tax treatment. It usually goes under the auspicious title of *net unrealized appreciation,* abbreviated simply as NUA.

Age 55–59½ Early Withdrawal Penalty Confusion

- If money comes directly from a benefit plan, such as a pension or 401(k) plan, then age 55 dictates.
- That is, there is a 10 percent early withdrawal penalty before age 55.
- If money comes directly from an IRA, like a rollover IRA or regular IRA, or 403(b) plan, then age 59½ dictates. That is, there is a 10 percent early withdrawal penalty before age 59½.

This taxation technique allows only the original cost of the stock to be immediately taxed, with the remaining appreciation taxed as capital gains. But, there are some tricky aspects to this method. First, any appreciation after distribution must wait until a year and a day for that portion to get the 20 percent long-term capital gains treatment. Second, you do have to pay ordinary tax on

Example

This tax analysis takes $300,000 in 401(k) employer stock and uses net unrealized appreciation (assuming analysis over 15 years, 7 percent investment returns, 36 percent tax bracket on stock cost basis, 28 percent tax bracket on IRA withdrawals):

- Immediate tax on stock cost basis is $36,000 and 20 percent capital gains on appreciation within 3 years is estimated at $42,000. Total taxes of $78,000.
  Result: Present value of taxes to be paid: *$70,100.*

- If rolled stock into IRA and anticipating withdrawals of $10,000 in each of 15 years, total taxes of $42,000.
  Result: Present value of taxes to be paid: *$25,500.*

Analysis. In this example, it is better to roll over stock into IRA than to use net unrealized appreciation. Total taxes paid and present value of taxes both favor rollover.

Caveat. Each situation would have differing stock cost basis, stock market value, marginal tax bracket, withdrawal needs, estimated timing when stock would be sold, and number of years used for planning.

the cost of the stock immediately, which could be a high tax year. Third, this requires an analysis of taxes projected to be paid over 10 to 15 years.

As a suggestion, if you anticipate selling the employer stock within a couple of years, you usually are better off not using net unrealized appreciation, but rather rolling the stock into an IRA and then taking money out of the IRA as you need it.

A host of organizations sponsor *403(b) plans:* colleges, private schools, hospitals and health centers, and nonprofit organizations. The most prominent 403(b) plan is TIAA-CREF, a college and private school fund. These plans generally pay out monthly payments, not lump sums. Payments are usually fully taxed as ordinary income (ask your organization if any amounts will be tax free).

If you've changed jobs, you will have a different 403(b) contract from each employer. One client had worked for four TIAA-CREF organizations and each contract specified the amount of that plan that could be paid as a lump sum, if any. The questions to ask are: What are your payment options, (including lump sums), your investment options, and your options to either roll over the plan into an IRA or to another 403(b) plan?

If you have the option of a lump sum, you can usually roll it entirely into an IRA. Your organization will confirm if that option exists. If you take it as a lump sum, however, you *cannot* use 10-Year Averaging, unlike 401(k) plans. This tax option has never been available to 403(b) plans.

The *457 plans* are actually deferred compensation plans of state and local governments. They have followed different sets of tax rules than pensions, 401(k), and 403(b) plans, however, beginning in 2002 they essentially will have the same distribution rules. They have similar contribution and investment features as their 401(k) and 403(b) counterparts, but they are almost always paid as monthly pensions.

The payments of 457 plans *cannot* use 10-Year Averaging. Distributions are ordinary income when paid.

SEP-IRA and SIMPLE-IRA plans are already IRAs, so there is little that needs to be done from a technical standpoint. You simply withdraw money when you need to and follow the standard IRA rules detailed later in this chapter.

Keogh plans can generally be either profit-sharing or money purchasing plans. Although arrangements can usually be made to pay as monthly amounts, in almost all cases they are rolled into IRAs and amounts are taken as needed.

Keogh plans are allowed to use the 10-Year Averaging tax treatment explained earlier. Although there are several other more technical rules, the two main criteria for using a Keogh plan are having been born before 1936 and not having used it previously.

Decisions and Distribution Rules for IRAs

IRAs have flexibility in that they can simply continue to grow tax-deferred and you can make withdrawals whenever you need the money. Typically, retirees roll over a lump sum from their pension, 401(k), 403(b), or 457 plan to an IRA.

Distributions from IRAs are generally taxable when received. For example, if you take a distribution of $10,000, that is added to your income and taxed at whatever tax rate would apply to your total income.

There are just a few exceptions. If you ever made any nondeductible contributions to an IRA (because you were not entitled to take a tax deduction), then a tax-free portion is calculated (on a percentage basis) each time until you've taken the full amount of the tax-free amount. Another exception involves the Roth IRA. Distributions of the amount of contributions are always tax free, as well as the earnings if held for 5 years and if over age 59½.

DEFINITIONS

ROLLOVER IRA
A tax-free exchange of money from one retirement plan to an IRA.

CONDUIT IRA
A tax-free rollover consisting of only one plan distribution. It can be rolled into another retirement plan, if allowed.

Also, it is a mistaken notion that all nondeductible IRAs should be aggregated (for tax purposes). If you've made contributions to both, regular and nondeductible IRAs, the first distributions must still account for partially tax-free withdrawals, regardless of where the distribution came from (regular or nondeductible).

IRAs can be rolled over to another IRA. If you don't like the investments or administration of an IRA, simply move it to another. There are two methods. First, have the IRA amount paid out to you and within 60 days roll it into another IRA. Second, have the IRA amount moved trustee-to-trustee, which is not technically considered a rollover.

The only rule to be aware of when moving IRA money to another is that if you move only a portion of IRA 1 to another IRA, then you cannot roll over any other money from IRA 1 within 12 months. But, if you do want to do several moves

Example

Calculate the tax-free amount on an IRA distribution where there were previous nondeductible contributions to IRAs:

Total amount in IRAs: $100,000

Amount of IRA withdrawal: $10,000

Amount of previous nondeductible IRAs: $4,000

Result: Tax-free amount of $10,000 distribution is 4 percent or *$400.*

Calculation: Divide the nondeductible amount by the total amount in IRAs: $4,000 divided by $100,000 equals 4 percent or $400 of the $10,000 distribution. Then subtract the $400 used from the original tax-free portion to determine how much is left for the next withdrawal, or $3,600. At the next distribution, divide $3,600 by the total in all IRAs to get the percentage and the amount of tax-free withdrawal. Repeat until the nondeductible amount of $4,000 is accounted for. Thereafter, all IRA distributions are fully taxable.

from IRA 1, then use the trustee-to-trustee moves as many times as you like to as many IRAs as you wish.

Penalties from IRAs

- Early withdrawal before 59½ (10 percent)
- Excess contributions (6 percent)
- Underwithdrawal at 70½ (50 percent)

The early withdrawal penalty might be familiar to most. It's an amount of 10 percent of any IRA withdrawals before age 59½. Here's how the penalty works. Let's say you took $10,000 from an IRA before you reached age 59½. Besides having to pay ordinary income tax on $10,000, you would have to pay 10 percent of the distribution as a penalty, or in this case $1,000. The penalty is shown on Form 5329.

The excess contribution penalty is for money put into an IRA that should not be. For example, if you made an overage contribution of $1,000, 6 percent of that excess amount is taxed as a penalty. It too is shown on Form 5329.

The underwithdrawal penalty is for money that should be withdrawn beginning at 70½ but is not. The penalty is 50 percent of the amount that should have been withdrawn. Use Form 5329, excess accumulations, to report.

There are several *exceptions to the 10 percent early withdrawal penalty:*

- If you are disabled, under a strict definition, which is the same as disability for Social Security.
- For unreimbursed medical expenses that exceed 7.5 percent of your adjusted gross income, up to the amount of the medical expense.
- For higher education expenses for yourself, spouse, children, or grandchildren.
- For first-time homebuyers or builders (up to a maximum of $10,000).
- For distributions from an inherited IRA.
- For distributions in the form of an annuity.

The annuity, or substantially equal payments exception, is often considered and sometimes used by early retirees. This annuity exception is calculated using life expectancy tables that would deplete the IRA over one's life expectancy, or joint life expectancy. However, these payments must be continued for the *longer* of 5 years or age 59½. For example, if a person started this method at age 57, it would have to continue for 5 years, or until age 62. The IRS also allows you to segregate an IRA specifically for this purpose; that is, you don't have to use all of your IRAs.

Three annuity calculation methods are permitted:

Method 1. Dividing the amount of an IRA by a life expectancy number, using the single or married tables, whichever applies. Table 9.1, in Chapter 9, is a single life expectancy table. If married, you can use the longer joint life expectancy tables shown in IRS Publication 590.

Method 2. Calculating an annuity amount using the previously mentioned tables and using a reasonable interest rate.

Method 3. Calculating an annuity amount using any reasonable life expectancy table and using any reasonable interest rate.

You can see the simplicity of Method 1, but Methods 2 and 3 result in higher withdrawal amounts. Whichever method you use, document the method and keep it with your tax records. If you want to increase the amount by inflation each year, you must make that part of your documented method. The IRS is very picky and will only permit the exact method you prescribed at the beginning. Any modification from the exact method could result in a penalty and the

Example

Person single, age 56, with IRA amount of $100,000.

Method 1. *$3,610* (using life expectancy of 27.7).

Method 2. *$8,269* (using a 7 percent interest rate along with the life expectancy of 27.7).

Method 3. *$9,040* (using a 7 percent interest rate and a life expectancy of 22 years).

unraveling of the whole approach. Again, if used, the method must be continued for the longer of 5 years or 59½.

What is the 70½ rule of IRAs? Beginning in 2001, there have been a number of changes in how to calculate the mandatory withdrawals from your IRAs starting at age 70½. In general, these rules have been greatly simplified and of course are greatly appreciated. You use a divisor based on a table shown in Chapter 9 (Table 9.3).

You total all of your IRAs (not Roth or Educational IRAs) for this purpose. Your "attained" age is used. That is, you will either attain age 70 or age 71 in the year you turn age 70½. Using the life expectancy table for a person age 70, the divisor is 26.2. The total of all IRAs as of January 1 (December 31 of previous year) is used and is simply divided by 26.2. That's the minimum withdrawal for a person, single or married.

You can either begin these minimum withdrawals by the end of the year when you turn age 70½ or you are allowed to delay the first withdrawal until April 1 of the following year. However, that second year you would also have to take out the second year's mandatory withdrawal by that December 31.

New as of 2001: Simplified rules for age 70½ minimum withdrawals for IRAs, 401(k)s, 403(b)s, 457s, and pensions. For most people, this means a little less needs to be withdrawn and importantly, there is now only one simple withdrawal method.

For example, if a person had IRAs totaling $50,000 and attained age 70, then the minimum withdrawal would be $1,908 ($50,000 divided by 26.2 equals $1,908).

The Roth IRA rules are greatly simplified from other IRAs for either early distributions and or those required for IRAs at 70½. You can also roll over a Roth IRA to another Roth.

First, withdrawals of your contributions are always tax free from a Roth, so if you need this money there's no tax or penalty at any time. However, if you exceed your contributions, then you need to wait five years from when you first made a Roth contribution and until age 59½ for that money. If you do take these earnings out early, then they are taxed as ordinary income plus a 10 percent penalty. The penalty is waived if you meet any of the exceptions listed previously for a regular IRA, such as disability, an annuity payment, and so forth.

Second, there are no required withdrawals at age 70½, or any age. Since they would be tax free, the IRS doesn't care how long they are in the Roth.

If you converted a regular IRA to a Roth IRA, all of your Roths are aggregated for tax purposes. First, distributions are tax free to the extent that there were (1) regular Roth contributions and (2) converted amounts, which, of course, had taxes assessed on the converted amounts. After contributions and converted amounts, earnings are tax free if held in the Roth for 5 years and until age 59½.

A Game Plan for Your Situation

Although there are myriad technical rules about benefit plans, they don't all apply to you. Thus, just check on the plans you have and you can ignore the rest of the chapter. But, even if you do get lost in some of the details, here's a suggestion: Keep the big picture in mind.

It's the big picture that allows you to keep all of your retirement resources in perspective. A client once was having difficulty in deciding which pension option she should take. It was not until we discussed all of her retirement income sources that she finally saw her pension as only a piece of her retirement puzzle. She thought that she had to select a lump sum from her pension because she wanted to leave something for her children. When we reviewed the value of her 401(k) plan, her other investments, and her house, she saw that her children would be well taken care of. It allowed her to select the higher single-life pension, with no survivor benefit, which she felt was best for her.

If you retire early, your pension and investments usually have to work harder for you because you're not yet collecting Social Security. Also, you may have a 10 percent early withdrawal penalty from IRAs or benefit plans. Here's where you have to devise two plans—one until you receive Social Security and one after.

Keeping Up to Date

One caveat is in order. This book is accurate as of the publishing date. I hope Congress (or the IRS through rulings) won't make changes before you need to use them (usually only a few changes are made each year).

CHAPTER 15

Step 4. In Retirement— Fine-Tuning Your Investments and Expenses

What to do in retirement, other than enjoy your new lifestyle? Keep your investments on track and make sure you don't overspend. Yes, you want to enjoy retirement, but your financial responsibilities, like life itself, haven't ended. No need for a big to-do. Just keep an eye on two things: investments and expenses. And there are only a few things you need to check on with each of them.

Tax Highlight				
INCOME TAX RATES TO DECLINE				
2000	2001	2002	. . .	2006
39.6%	39.1%	38.6%		35%
36	35.5	35		33
31	30.5	30		28
28	27.5	27		25
15	refund credit	10–15		10–15

The Investment Answer

Let's explore investments first, because they're more complicated. Why? For several reasons: (1) You will probably have a different asset allocation from when you were working; (2) you will probably focus on income, which you didn't do when working; and (3) you will still have a component of growth in your portfolio, because retirement will probably continue for a fairly long time and you'll want to stay ahead of inflation.

Here is the *ideal retirement portfolio,* a ready-made portfolio that is sophisticated in all regards; the only thing it lacks is pizazz, which may be precisely what you want in retirement. It's not that this portfolio is ideal for everyone, but it is the ideal starting point for your thinking:

The Ideal Retirement Investment Portfolio

- 35 percent is in stocks, of which:

    —90 percent is in large domestic stocks.

    —5 percent is in small cap stocks.

    —5 percent is in international stocks.

- 65 percent is in bonds and money market funds, of which:

    —80 percent is in short-term and/or intermediate bonds.

    —20 percent is in money market funds.

Why is this the ideal portfolio? Because it is on the conservative side and it focuses on income. It should provide you on average about 5 percent in income and 3 percent in growth—or a total return each year of about 8 percent. The income comes mainly from bonds but stocks do provide some income in dividends. The growth is assumed to come only from stocks. If you take the growth out as "income," then you'll be able to take out as much as 8 percent a year and maintain your portfolio's value. Because the stock market is a little unpredictable, you'll have to settle for more in some years, less in others. But on average, this is a portfolio that retirees can live with long term.

There are several ways to construct the portfolio. The easiest and simplest is to find a balanced mutual fund that mirrors this approximate 35 percent allocation in stocks and 65 percent in bonds and put all your money in it. An example is Vanguard's Wellesley fund with 35 to 40 percent in stocks. It may be just a titch high on stocks, but it's definitely in the ballpark. You or your broker can construct the same portfolio with individual funds and/or stocks. Just keep the overall 35/65 percentage and have the interest and dividends sent to you each month.

To see this in actual numbers, here are the Wellesley's returns for the past 10 years, which would typify a 35/65 percentage portfolio performance:

YEAR	(%)	YEAR	(%)
1991	21.4	1996	9.4
1992	8.7	1997	20.2
1993	14.6	1998	11.8
1994	−4.4	1999	−4.1
1995	28.9	2000	16.2

Even this conservative portfolio has considerable volatility to it. (Imagine the volatility of a portfolio with a higher percentage in stocks.) So, in good years you leave some of the extra growth in the portfolio and in lean years you dip into principal. Overall, you meet your conservative objectives of income and growth.

To cement this point, remember in Chapter 3, the worst years for the stock market were shown (Table 3.1). Table 15.1 shows 2 of those 7 years.

The first year is 1974, the worst year for the market since the Depression. In 1974, inflation shot up mainly from OPEC gas prices and forced long lines to buy gas around the country. But a conservative portfolio only suffered a tolerable −5 percent. Although you give up the higher stock market returns in good years, you only suffer small losses in bad years. That's the point for retirees: a more stable portfolio with an emphasis on income.

I'm writing this book in the middle of 2001, so I don't know what the second half will bring (the first half was about flat overall). But last year, 2000, was a

TABLE 15.1 The Worst Investment Years

	100% STOCKS 0% BONDS	80% STOCKS 20% BONDS	65% STOCKS 35% BONDS	35% STOCKS 65% BONDS
1974	−26.5%	−20.0%	−15.2%	−5.5%
2000	−9.1	−4.8	−1.5	5.0

down year for the market, on average about −9 percent (those who were highly invested in tech stocks suffered 50 percent or more in losses). But, if you were invested in our conservative portfolio, you would have seen a actual increase of about 5 percent. Why such an increase? Because bonds did very well in 2000 with interest rates declining.

How would you *calibrate this allocation for yourself*? If you need even higher income with a more stable portfolio, you could increase the percentage of bonds (lowering the percentage of stocks), so you could have a higher income with an even more stable overall portfolio. Alternatively, if you feel inclined to have more growth, you could increase the percentage of stocks.

Another way to affect the volatility of the portfolio is to invest in higher risk stocks, smaller cap, or sector stocks like technology, and international stocks. A higher percentage of these can boost the performance in some years and deflate it further in others.

However, a *too conservative portfolio* can be dangerous. One retired family in the late 1980s thought that they were well protected because they had all their money in long-term CDs earning 10 percent. However, when the CDs finally came due, they panicked because they could only get 5 percent on new CDs. Their income crashed overnight by 50 percent! Some conservative portfolio.

Now, let's turn to *bonds,* the 65 percent, or so, in the portfolio. As explained in Chapter 3, bonds are long-term investments that pay a fixed interest. But bonds come in many maturities. Some are as short as 2 to 3 years, some are called intermediate and are 5 to 10 years, and the longest are 25 and 30 years. (There are actually a few that are 100 years.)

You could buy individual bonds or bond funds, or a combination. Individual bonds offer stability of value if you hold them to maturity. Bond funds offer flexibility of income in that you can simply instruct the fund to send you "x" number of dollars each month, even if that amount is more than the actual interest. With individual bonds, you would have to sell some to receive more than the actual interest.

A popular bond strategy is a *staggered ladder of maturities.* It can effectively stabilize your portfolio while still capturing the average interest rate across a number of maturities.

The ladder doesn't have to be for the whole portfolio, but for a portion, say 50 percent to 80 percent. That would leave some for money market funds for liquidity. It can easily be accomplished with corporate bonds or Treasury notes. Although there is some talk of eliminating government notes and bonds with the potential high surpluses, at the moment you could buy notes, say in 2-, 5-, and 10-year maturities.

This laddering approach has at least two advantages: (1) It allows you to take advantage of interest rates at various maturities, and (2) it takes all the anguish out of deciding what to do with a maturing note. Always "go long" to keep the ladder staggered; that is, buy a 10-year note with the maturing amount.

Income can come from *interest* and/or *capital gains*. The obvious way to collect income is to simply let the income of your investments flow to you. However, another way of getting income is to take out the gains each year. Or, you can approximate how much you can take out on average to keep your portfolio about even over the long term.

To *monitor your investments* you can turn back to Chapter 3, where this was explained in some detail. However, in general, you compare your portfolio against what a similar stock, bond, and money market portfolio did. If you did not keep up, you may need to adjust some specific securities or funds that were poor performers.

When do you go to this more conservative portfolio? I recommend making the adjustment several years before you retire. That way, you're all set as you enter retirement. Also, you don't want a market downturn just before you retire to disrupt your retirement plans.

So, the main thing to do in retirement with respect to your investments: Keep an eye on your allocation and on those more volatile stocks.

Example

STAGGERED LADDER OF MATURITIES OF NOTES ($100,000 IN BONDS)

$20,000 in 2-year notes

$20,000 in 3-year notes

$20,000 in 5-year notes

$20,000 in 7-year notes

$20,000 in 10-year notes

Advantage. You capture interest rates across several maturities.

Method. In two years when the first note matures, buy a 10-year note to keep the ladder intact.

The Expense Answer

If you've done your homework and know your expenses, you actually can simplify your chore in retirement. How? By only tracking a few key expense categories. Because most of your costs will be stable, like groceries, clothes, rent, or real estate taxes, you only need to monitor those categories that could create problems for you, such as eating out and travel.

It may take you a year or two in retirement to identify stable and unstable categories. Let's say that travel is a category that you think could balloon out of control. Then, set a budget for that item, and as you go through the year only keep track of that total. No need to monitor the expenses that remain stable. (You probably have better things to do.)

My good friend, Frank Hardy, has identified other items that could spiral out of hand. "In my experience with retirees, any or all of these could be a problem: hobbies, computers and home entertainment centers, cost of cars, redecorating, and home improvements."

Then, every three to five years, you may wish to again repeat the task of completing the expense worksheet in its entirety (Figure 7.2), just to verify each category.

Another way to monitor your expenses is to assess your total investment portfolio at the end of each year. Is there a particular decrease that hasn't been accounted for by investments? It's probably a particular expense category, perhaps temporary, but it's the time for you to determine its cause. It could also mean that the culprit may be across the board in many categories. Then it's time to redo your expenses and set a strict budget for yourself.

Inflation moves relentlessly along. If your expenses experienced a 2 percent increase each year, they would double in 35 years. If 3 percent, they would double after 23 years. So, if your expenses started at retirement, at, say, $60,000, and inflation increased on average at 3 percent, then your expenses would have increased to $120,000 in 23 years.

Are you on a fixed income? Some retirees with an emphasis on pensions, which hardly ever have inflation increases, will have that portion fixed. Social Security has automatic inflation increases each year.

How Long Will It Last? That's probably the number one question people have (besides "how long will I last"). You don't want to take too much out of your retirement resources too early, nor too fast. But investments are there for your financial well-being and can be touched as long as you do it prudently.

TABLE 15.2 Depleting a Lump Sum—How Long Will It Last? (Assuming 3 Percent Increasing Amounts)

WITHDRAWAL RATE	INVESTMENT RATE						
	4%	5%	6%	7%	8%	10%	12%
5%	25	27	30	40	—	—	—
6%	19	20	25	30	38	—	—
7%	15	18	20	23	25	35	—
8%	14	15	17	19	20	30	—
9%	12	13	15	15	17	25	—
10%	11	12	13	14	15	20	25
12%	9	10	10	11	12	14	17
15%	7	8	8	9	9	10	11

Tables 15.2, 15.3, and 15.4 can help you answer how long a nest egg would last if you wanted to use it up. Each table has the same information but presents it differently, depending on what question you need answered. Table 15.2 answers how many years it would last; Table 15.3 answers what withdrawal rate is sustainable; and Table 15.4 shows what investment rate makes it work. The answer is rounded to the nearest even percentage or year. Each table assumes

TABLE 15.3 Depleting a Lump Sum—What Withdrawal Rate? (Assuming 3 Percent Increasing Amounts)

INVESTMENT RATE	YEARS						
	10	15	20	25	30	35	40
4%	11%	7%	6%	5%	4%	3%	—
5%	12	8	6	5	5	4	3%
6%	12	9	7	6	5	4	4
7%	13	9	8	7	6	5	5
8%	13	10	8	7	6	6	6
10%	15	11	10	9	8	8	7
12%	16	13	11	10	9	9	9
15%	18	15	13	13	12	12	12

TABLE 15.4 Depleting a Lump Sum—What Investment Rate? (Assuming 3 Percent Increasing Amounts)

WITHDRAWAL RATE	YEARS						
	10	15	20	25	30	35	40
5%	—	—	3%	4%	6%	6%	7%
6%	—	2%	5	6	7	8	8
7%	—	4	7	8	9	10	10
8%	—	5	8	10	10	11	11
10%	3%	9	11	12	13	13	13
12%	6	12	12	14	15	15	15
15%	10	15	17	17	17	18	18

that whatever amount you start with is to be increased by 3 percent a year to keep up with inflation.

The resultant number in Table 15.2 is the years your lump sum would last given specific investment and withdrawal rates. If you had, say, $100,000 and wanted to know how long it could last if it earned 8 percent and you took a withdrawal rate of 10 percent, (starting at $10,000 a year, increasing by 3 percent inflation each year), well the answer is: 15 years.

The resultant percentage shown in Table 15.3 is the withdrawal rate of the lump sum given the desired number of years and investment rate. If you had $100,000 and wanted it to last 20 years and it was estimated to earn 8 percent, what could be the withdrawal rate? Answer: 8 percent. An 8 percent withdrawal rate would be permitted of the initial $100,000, which would be $8,000, and it would increase by a 3 percent rate of inflation. The lump sum would last 20 years under this circumstance.

The resultant percentage in Table 15.4 is the investment rate a lump sum must earn given a desired number of years and withdrawal rate. If you had a lump sum of $100,000 and wanted it to last 25 years, and you wanted to take out withdrawals beginning at 8 percent, or $8,000, increasing 3 percent for inflation each year, how much would the lump sum need to earn? Answer: 10 percent.

Life expectancy is part of this planning. Discussed in Chapter 9, the relevance of a long life is a need to extend our investment portfolios beyond our 80s. Although it's suggested that you use age 90 as a general planning age for how long you'll live, once you approach 90, you'll have to start increasing your planning horizon to a longer number, perhaps 95 or longer.

Your *IRAs at age 70½* have to start to be withdrawn (see Chapter 14). So, this is another financial chore to keep your eye on. Although the IRS has expressed an interest in keeping the rules as they are now for quite some time, it would be good to obtain IRS publication 590 just as you approach this age. Also, keep in mind that only a minimum withdrawal is required, which you might be doing anyway. You only need to take out about 4 percent for the first several years.

Summary

Keep your eye on your overall investment results and a few critical expense categories. If you have to work to earn extra money, you'll be among the growing number doing the same thing. But outside of that, you should be able to concentrate on enjoying your new lifestyle.

CHAPTER 16

Estate Planning, Long-Term Care, and Leaving Money

A funny thing happened on with way to eliminating the estate tax. We're not sure it's been eliminated. To meet differing perceptions about the potential budget surpluses, Congress reduced this tax down to zero by 2010, but if it's not reinstated, it will go back to where it would have been at that time, namely only a $1 million exclusion per person.

So, under these circumstances, what can you assume and how can you deal with estate planning? First, determine if these changes will mean anything to you. If you have less than $1 million in your estate, then there is nothing to do, because these changes will not affect you one way or another.

If you have over $1 million, especially $2 million or more, then you can plan for the eventual $2 and $3.5 million increases in exclusion, but don't assume that the tax will be zero until it is. Then, in 2011, or earlier, if Congress makes these changes permanent, revisit your estate plan.

Even if the estate tax goes to zero, a trap is lurking behind the scenes for larger estates. There may be *capital gain taxes,* and significant taxes at that, where none existed before. Before these changes, heirs received assets with the tax basis at current market values. This is known as receiving an asset with a stepped-up basis. If the heirs sold any stocks or mutual funds the next day, there would be no taxes. They would be able to keep all the money.

Tax Highlight

NEW FEDERAL ESTATE TAXES

Increased Exclusion:

2002—$1 million

2004—$1.5 million

2006—$2 million

2009—$3.5 million

Decreased Rates:

2002—top rate is 50 percent

2003—2007 top rate is reduced 1 percent a year to 45 percent

Estate Tax (and Generation-Skipping Tax) Eliminated   2010

Add on for tax basis: $3 million for spouses and $1.3 for other heirs

Need for Congress to renew   2011

Now, the heirs would receive stocks and mutual funds with the owner's original tax basis! This is not a trivial matter. Result: Heirs could owe significant capital gain taxes when they sell any asset. The federal government would then keep 20 percent (the long-term capital gains tax rate) of the inherited assets and the states could also extract their share. Estate tax planning would then become capital gain planning.

As relief to most spouses and heirs, the new tax law specifies that there will be a $3 million add-on to the tax basis of inherited assets for spouses and $1.3 million for all other heirs.

Another aspect of estate taxes will come to the fore: No longer will the little noticed IRD come into play, which will cause income tax where some relief still exists today. This is discussed later in this chapter under the title *Income in Respect to a Decedent (IRD)*.

The Basics of Estate Planning:
Wills and Will Substitutes

The *will is the basic document of estate planning.* This is a legal document that specifies what is to be done with our assets and our property on our death (those that are not taken care of by other means). Assets with named beneficiaries or assets owned jointly with rights of survivorship automatically pass to someone else. A will would only direct other assets.

But the will specifies the person you trust to manage the affairs of your estate and to see that all your wishes are carried out. This person is called the *executor,* or sometimes the *personal representative.* (Let's rid ourselves of the term *executrix,* which had been the term for a female executor.) Importantly for young couples, the will also names guardians for their minor children, if that becomes necessary.

Each *state has its own rules about wills.* These rules indicate how many witnesses are necessary and what forms are acceptable. Most states require two or three witnesses and stipulate whether *handwritten (holographic) wills* are acceptable. Each state also has individual laws relating to wills and estates with no two states exactly alike. If you move to another state, be sure to have an estate lawyer in the new state verify whether the intents stated in your will and other estate documents still stand under the new state. For example, a person moved to Wisconsin who had named his brother, who lived in Texas, as his executor. Wisconsin, however, requires that the executor be a Wisconsin resident. Without checking, the person thought that his will would do what he intended, when in fact his brother was an invalid executor.

A *codicil* is a change, or amendment, to a will. It must be done as formally as the will itself.

Sometimes, *personal instruction papers* are part of estate planning. They are expressed wishes that are not generally covered in a will, for example, if you want to be cremated or where you wanted to be buried.

The Last Will and Testament

The word *will* is an English term referring to the disposition of real property, like land and buildings, in other words, real estate. *Testament* comes from the Latin and refers to the disposition of personal property, which is everything other than real estate. Thus, the term *Last Will and Testament* refers to the disposing of all property, real and personal. The modern definition of will blends both meanings of real and personal property into the one familiar word.

Now, a *medical or health proxy* is becoming a standard estate-planning step. It expresses your desire for sustaining your life under all circumstances, or your wishes not to be resuscitated.

A *power of attorney* is an important document for people who are too ill to manage their own financial affairs. Technically called a "durable" power of attorney, it stays in effect even after one becomes incapacitated. It is being used with increasing frequency for elderly parents.

Having *no will* at the time of death is called dying "intestate." That doesn't mean that the state would get your money. It means that it would fall back to the state to specify who receives your assets that are not passed automatically. Typically, a state designates either that a spouse and children would divide the estate one-half—one-half, or one-third—two-thirds.

Under state law, you cannot disinherit your spouse or children. In those cases, the court allows assets to be redirected to spouses and children.

Probate is the process of proving in court that a will is valid and then overseeing the distribution of assets. Usually each county of a state has a probate or surrogate court that handles these matters, in addition to overseeing trusts, guardianships, and receiverships. These courts are there to decide those cases where family disputes arise. The same court also appoints substitute executors or guardians if they are necessary.

States sometimes set the amounts executors may charge for handling estate matters. This is usually a percentage of the estate value; typically it could be 5 percent on the first $100,000, 4 percent up to $500,000, and 3 percent up to $1 million or more.

Will substitutes are assets passing outside the will. These assets, especially those with a named beneficiary, pass to someone automatically. The three common will substitutes are: *joint ownership with rights of survivorship,* sometimes abbreviated as JOWROS, named *beneficiaries,* and *trusts.*

Joint ownership itself can take several forms. Under *joint ownership with rights of survivorship,* property passes automatically to the other owner at the time of death. It's assumed that each survivor owns 100 percent. Even if your will specified someone other than the person with the rights of survivorship, it wouldn't matter because having rights of survivorship takes precedence over a will. A special form of joint ownership with rights of survivorship in some states is called *Tenants by the Entirety,* such as in New Jersey. It pertains to property owned only between spouses.

Under *tenants in common,* your will would specify who would receive your share of the property. If you bought a boat with your sister and she contributed

30 percent, your will would need to specify who receives your 70 percent. Your sister doesn't automatically get your share.

A named *beneficiary* is a common form of will substitute. Life insurance, IRAs, 401(k), 403(b)s, and other benefit plans usually have a named beneficiary. That beneficiary would automatically receive the asset at the death of the owner. (By law, a named beneficiary takes precedence over a will.) If the beneficiary is no longer alive when the owner dies (because the owner forgot to rename the beneficiary), then it becomes part of the estate and the owner's will designates who receives these assets.

A *contingent beneficiary* is often named for this reason, in case the primary beneficiary(s) is not alive.

A *trust* is another will substitute. The subject of wills, joint ownership of property, and estate and inheritance taxes may be complicated enough, but the subject of trusts makes the entire estate planning business seem beyond most people. It need not be, since a trust can be a good and sensible vehicle for some people.

Trusts are legal documents *governed by state law.* They are written with *specific provisions,* reflecting the desires of the person setting up the trust. Thus, a trust can be a unique document, or it can take on a common form that has evolved over time through experience and use. Some, with special characteristics or functions, have specific names like Clifford or Totten, or they are named after their IRS code section, for example, 2503(c) Trusts (for kids).

Most trusts allow the person who set up the trust the right to control the assets. This includes even changing the trust agreement or canceling it. This trust is appropriately called a *revocable* trust.

Before you set up a trust, you will want to know the initial cost and the potential ongoing costs and fees for the management of the assets. This would include the initial legal documents, the preparation of tax returns (if any), and the general fees of ongoing investments and management. Trusts can cost $1,000 or more to set up and 1 percent of the assets as an ongoing management fee.

A *bypass trust,* also called a *credit shelter trust,* is the most common trust set up today for couples. It utilizes

DEFINITIONS

REVOCABLE TRUST
One that you can change.

IRREVOCABLE TRUST
One that you can't change once set up. Since it can't be changed, the person who set it up doesn't own the assets and thus can reduce his or her eventual estate taxes.

LIVING TRUST
One that is in effect while you are still living.

TESTAMENTARY TRUST
One that is usually written into your will and takes effect at your death.

the individual estate tax exclusion for each spouse to minimize estate taxes. The couple needs to own typically $1.5 to $2 million in assets for this arrangement to work.

It is aptly named bypass because the assets bypass the surviving spouse's estate for estate tax purposes. Assets up to the prevailing exclusion ($1 million in 2002) are put into the trust at the first spouse's death and pay income to the surviving spouse for however long that spouse lives. Then, the assets are distributed to children (or others) as specified by the trust. In this way, assets in the bypass trust become free of estate taxes in either spouse's estate. They meet the exclusion of the spouse who died and since the trust assets are not owned by the surviving spouse, they are not included in the estate whenever the second spouses dies.

For spouses, a few cautions on bypass trusts are in order. Often IRAs, benefit plans, or the couple's residence are the main (if not sole) assets, which may not be appropriate for these trusts. Further, a surviving spouse may want to control the assets, not just receive the income. Surviving spouses should be able to decide how much, if any, money or assets should go into the trust when the other spouse dies.

In the past, it was common to set up a *marital trust.* This was a trust created through the will at death to pay income to the surviving spouse. This was done to protect the surviving spouse, traditionally the wife who was unfamiliar with finance. With women becoming as versed in finance as men, or even more so, these trusts are now seen as a relic of the past.

State Estate and Inheritance Taxes

Not all states impose a separate estate tax, and in fact states have been busy repealing these taxes, where they existed, before the federal government even thought about it. For those states that still do, there are usually two types: an "estate tax" and an "inheritance tax." For estate taxes, like the federal system, all assets are added up and after certain exclusions, for administration expenses and such, a tax is determined. In an inheritance tax system, the amount of the tax is determined by who gets the money. Money going to a spouse or children, for example, would be taxed at a lower rate, than for brothers and sisters or others. Usually there are several categories, or classes, of beneficiaries and a different tax is prescribed for each.

Historically, the community-property states have been California, Nevada, Arizona, New Mexico, and Texas (all in the southwest) and Louisiana (although Louisiana law is from old French law). Washington and Idaho are also community-property states, as is Wisconsin, which adopted it to reflect the modern notion in divorce that each spouse should have half of the property.

The new tax law doesn't change the *annual gift of $10,000* to individuals each year (both spouses can give a combined $20,000). It will still be excluded from estate/gift taxes.

Rules and Taxes on Inheriting IRAs and Benefit Plans

There is a key tax area in estate planning that usually gets overlooked: inheriting money in an IRA or benefit plan. Reviewing it may help you focus on the importance of naming beneficiaries to those that you own. And, if you inherit an IRA or benefit plan that caused estate taxes, you have an extremely important tax deduction coming when you take distributions: It's abbreviated as IRD and is explained later.

A few basics are in order. First, an IRA or benefit plan is owned only by the owner. No joint ownership is allowed. You name a beneficiary(s) who would receive it after your death. Although an estate can be named as the beneficiary, that is usually ill advised because income taxes would be due immediately instead of across many years as for a person. Second, spouses can roll the money into their own IRA, or not, giving them more flexibility in withdrawing.

A *spouse* inheriting an IRA, 401(k), 403(b), pension plan, and other qualified plan, can roll the plan into her or his own IRA or leave it in the inherited IRA. If it was rolled over, then the spouse can delay any required withdrawals until reaching 70½. If it was left in the inherited IRA, the spouse can wait until the deceased spouse would have been 70½ and then take out minimum distributions based on the surviving spouse's age.

A *nonspouse*, like a child, sister, or friend, can continue the deferral, but must start taking minimum distributions by the end of the year following the owner's death. Otherwise, all the money must be distributed within 5 years. An

> **DEFINITIONS**
>
> **COMMON-LAW STATES**
> Those states that follow old English law.
>
> **COMMUNITY-PROPERTY STATES**
> Those states that follow old Spanish law. A community-property state, in general, assumes that each spouse owns one-half of all assets, except for those assets earned while single or received through inheritance, as long as those assets are kept separate.

IRA that is inherited by a nonspouse is called, appropriately, an *inherited IRA*. It must remain in the owner's name and cannot be put in the beneficiary's name. (If you did put your name on it, the entire balance could become taxable.) It can, however, be moved to another financial institution, which is suggested if it has better investments or gives you more flexible distribution options.

If the deceased person started the age 70½ withdrawals, then you can continue the withdrawals, but at your own life expectancy.

For a *Roth IRA,* there are no 70½ rules, when the owner must take money out, as opposed to regular IRAs. However, *beneficiaries* of Roth IRAs must follow similar rules for regular IRAs: They must start taking money out by December 31 following the year of death, otherwise within 5 years. Because there are no required age 70½ withdrawals for an owner, a beneficiary of a Roth IRA, whether before or after the owner's age 70½, simply follows the rules of December 31, or 5 years. Also, a spouse can roll the Roth into one of his or her own.

Income in Respect to a Decedent (IRD)

It's surprising how little this technical gem, called IRD for short, is known, but it can save a significant amount of income taxes for heirs where estate taxes had to be paid under today's estate tax structure.

If estate taxes had to be paid because of the value of IRAs, 401(k)s, and other pension plans, there is a dollar-for-dollar tax deduction when distributions are taken by heirs (or by estates if necessary). Since income taxes are almost always due for heirs when they take distributions from IRAs, 401(k)s, other pensions, and so forth (just as they were for the owner), this has the result of offsetting the estate taxes paid on these assets.

To arrive at the amount that can be offset, two calculations are performed: the actual amount of estate taxes and the amount of taxes if there were no IRAs or benefit plans. The difference between the two is the amount of taxable distributions to heirs that can be taken as tax deductions in their taxes. It's actually taken as a 2 percent miscellaneous deduction, without the 2 percent hurdle, for each dollar that is taxed.

As an example, if the amount of estate tax that was paid for these plans was $100,000, then the first $100,000 of taxable IRA, and other plans, withdrawn by heirs receives a deduction dollar-for-dollar. Thus, the estate tax is thereby re-couped by the tax deduction.

If the estate tax is eliminated, however, then there will be no more IRD, and heirs will have to pay all of the income taxes due on these distributions. This, along with the hidden capital gains tax that could pop up for larger estates, guarantees that taxes of one sort or another will still be paid in conjunction with a person's death.

If You Remarry

After a lifetime of accumulating assets, *prenuptial agreements* are recom-mended if you remarry. This assures that children will receive their share of their parents' assets. After all, marriages in retirement may not last forever. If however, the marriage has lasted for at least 5 years and the couple wants to plan for their potential physical and mental deterioration, then the couple may want to look anew at their wills and other arrangements, such as giving power of attorney over each other's finances.

Long-Term Care Insurance

Until medicine comes to our rescue, we will have a high probability of reaching a point in our lives where we become truly old and infirm. This may mean con-finement to a wheelchair, perhaps to a bed. Nursing home care could be our final milieu. But Medicare doesn't currently pay for this care, whether in a nursing home or in your home. Medicaid does, but the program is designed for the poor. For those who won't be in the poor category, there's long-term care insurance. The decision is whether to buy this insurance or self-insure.

Averages may not apply to individuals very well, but some averages can be helpful. On average, a person will need to enter a nursing home after age 85 and be there for 3 years. The average annual cost of a nursing home is about $50,000, higher in urban areas, lower in rural areas.

Prime candidates for long-term care insurance are those with between $70,000 and $1 million in investments. Below $70,000 you should be covered by Medicaid. Above $1 million you may decide to self-insure.

If you are considering this insurance, keep in mind two basics: you will need to pass a physical and premiums are higher the older you are (see Table 16.1).

TABLE 16.1 Average Annual Premiums for Long-Term Care Insurance (For Policies That Pay $100 a Day and 5 Percent Compounded Inflation Protection)

AGE WHEN PREMIUMS START	3-YEAR COVERAGE	4-YEAR COVERAGE
50	$ 600	$ 888
60	932	1,400
70	1,725	2,590
79	3,684	5,880

Also, a comprehensive long-term care insurance policy should cover services in a nursing home, at-home care, adult day services, or assisted living.

Leaving Money

There are at least three philosophies about leaving money to children: They should get every cent, they should get enough to make their lives a little more comfortable, or they should get as little as possible because they could lose motivation to attain a successful life on their own. Whichever philosophy you adopt, I strongly recommend that you should not deprive yourself of your deserved retirement lifestyle, just to make sure your children get the maximum inheritance.

It may be generational, but many of the Depression/War people want to give as much as possible to their children. Perhaps their early experiences of having next to nothing still direct their actions. They have money and they want to share it with their children, even if their children are well-off. They also may feel as if they are communicating that they are successful when they give money to their children and grandchildren.

The Balance generation seems more ambivalent. If they have money to give fine, but they want to make sure they are fine first. It's too early to detect the baby boomers' attitudes on this subject, but they may continue the trend away from automatically giving children whatever they need.

Some people feel more inclined to give money—if they are going to do so—while they are still alive. That way, they not only can enjoy being with their children and grandchildren, but can enjoy seeing the benefits of the gifts to them.

Finally, if you are single and have no children, charities can be an ideal target of your eventual estate, especially if you have a special charity in mind.

Summary

To complete your retirement planning, review the various aspects of estate planning. Make sure your will, power of attorney, and health proxy are all up-to-date and express your current wishes. Make changes as your situation and thinking change. Although denial about disability in old age and your eventual death may have been appropriate earlier in your life, now is the time to overcome that denial and think through the last part of your life.

As for the new tax law, assume that the increases in estate exclusion will occur, but along about 2010, revisit this subject. The elimination of estate taxes may or not happen, either in 2011, or earlier, if the budget surpluses continue to materialize. And even if they do, then your planning hasn't ended: you may then have to strategize about capital gains.

CHAPTER 17

The Chase Is Over: How You Can Enjoy Retirement Once There

A day without the hassle of the commute. Without the crush of deadlines getting those reports in. In retirement, if you listen—because you now can— you can actually hear the almost silent whirl of the fan inside the computer cooling the master chip.

Above all, the workaday tensions slowly melt away. It takes from one day to six months. You have your life back. Now what? The one universal comment people have given since I started asking "What does retirement mean to you?" is, "It's a time of my life when I can do what I want, how I want, and when I want."

After hearing people try to define retirement for almost 20 years, I conclude that the most appropriate individual and universal definition is encapsulated in a single word: *possibilities.* My daughter, who is a junior in college, sees the world as possibilities, which will inevitably narrow as she progresses through life and finds bumps in the road. But with retirement comes another chance to open our imaginations and think of possibilities.

Getting Started

Where to Start? Ask yourself this question: *What does retirement mean to you?*
Here's what some have said:

"Spending more time with my grandkids."

"Can travel and don't have to rush home."

"Don't have to battle traffic everyday."

"Can work in my garden."

"Being able to sleep late."

"Able to read a book cover-to-cover in one sitting."

"Work in the local hardware store."

"Open up an art gallery."

Let me state my bias up front. Many options are available: taking care of your grandchildren, tending to your garden, learning the wisdom of Socrates, performing in an orchestra, traveling to an unfamiliar place, volunteering in a hospital, or continuing to work for pay. To me, all of these are equally valid, equally inspiring, and equally noble for the person who chooses to do them. For each individual, they are the guarantees of life's possibilities.

Although we have stereotypes about what retired people should do, retirement doesn't come with instructions. And more and more people tend to ignore the stereotypes anyway and, like Robert Frost, travel their own chosen road. People are seeing retirement, like life itself, as a journey.

A couple of years ago at a seminar, a middle-aged woman explained how she was going to take piano lessons and join an orchestra when she retired. People were in awe and said, "Now there's a retirement!" At the same seminar, a middle-aged man volunteered that he was going to spend time with his grandchildren, and another woman was looking forward to digging in her garden. Why shouldn't grandchildren and gardens take center stage in our lives and be just as noble?

As soon as you mention to your family, friends, and work associates that you might be retiring, they often offer well-meaning suggestions: "You should go back to school," "Now you can travel to our national parks," "Now you can volunteer at the hospital."

Remember who gave you which specific suggestion. People tend to project on others what they want to do themselves. So, when they retire, you can feed back their suggestions to them, where they belong.

For you, look to yourself. Create your own retirement. Yes, listen to what others may suggest, but above all, listen to what lies inside you—your dreams, your desires—and begin to make them a reality.

Where to Live?

A couple came up to me during a break at a seminar in Princeton, New Jersey. Martha said that she wanted to stay in Princeton when they retired, but Henry wanted to move to Florida. They didn't know what to do. Could I please decide this for them?

After a moment of dramatic thought, I said to them, that it's not unusual to arrive at retirement with two separate plans. People are busy and often haven't had the time to discuss these ideas with each other. We sometimes make too many assumptions, without discussion.

My suggestion to them was to start over without the Princeton/Florida conclusion. They could begin by discussing what it is about Princeton and Florida that attracted them to these places. For Martha, it was family and culture. For Henry, it was deep-sea fishing. Well, how could they accomplish both of these? Sometime later, they called with their plan. It was six months in Princeton and six months in a college town in North Carolina, not too far from family and ocean fishing.

Housing Options

- *Staying put.* The majority stay right where they are. They know the community, have their doctors, and are close to their children.

- *Moving to a warmer climate.* This is a common change for those in winter climes. Rent before buying. Advantages are new place, new adventures, and pleasant weather.

- *Snow bird.* If you can afford it! It allows for a retreat from shoveling snow, but keeps you connected to your hometown. You have the variety of two communities and two sets of friends.

- *Condo or co-op.* It eliminates cutting the grass and maximizes your personal time.

- *Adult community.* Places range from an active lifestyle to a prenursing home. People either love or hate them, with few feeling neutral.

Want to hear an unusual approach to where to live? Throughout Bill's career, he and his wife Kate, moved from one oil refinery to another—three or four years at a location and then on the next engineering assignment. In retirement, did they want to travel anymore? Actually, yes! However, they now wanted to live where they chose.

First, they were going to move to Martha's Vineyard. They had always wanted to live there. Then, every three or four years, they were going to move to another place they always dreamed of. San Francisco, Hawaii, and Key West were on their list.

Charlie and Sharon lived in sunny California. Where were they going to retire? Alaska of course. They had a cabin close to Juneau, and they had been going there on vacation for many years. They also had a long list of friends who wanted to visit them. Their solution was not for everyone, but it shows how you can rethink this whole business of where to live.

If you're among the adventuresome few, your retirement fantasy may pull you abroad, to Mexico, Costa Rica, Portugal, or Provence. Before you set roots, a liberal testing of the location is an absolute must. Find any Americans in the area to explore the potential problems and pitfalls, including the currency. A number of years ago, the Mexican peso devalued many Americans' peso deposits. In terms of taxes, you are still taxed by Uncle Sam on your investment income, pensions, and IRA withdrawals, but you get a break on the first $78,000 of earned income in 2001 and $80,000 in 2002—that's salary income. Many countries may also tax you, so homework is needed. IRS Publications 593 (Tax Highlights for U.S. Citizens and Residents Going Abroad) and 901 (U.S. Treaties) are must reading. To order from the IRS, call 800/TAX-3676.

What to Do?

This is the story of Joe. When he retired, he settled in his rocking chair on his big Victorian porch. For almost six months, he just rocked back and forth for most of his waking hours. Family, friends, and neighbors were starting to worry about Joe. But one day he got off that rocking chair and busied himself with all kinds of things. What happened?

He said, "I never was retired, and didn't know what to do. I was simply thinking what I was going to do and once I got it figured out, then I did it." Like Joe, you may need some time to think about what to do in retirement.

Just take a little time, and you'll be busier than ever. Retirees have observed that, if you're an active person you'll be active in retirement. Also, those who retire "to" retirement will find the transition easier, than those who retire "from" their jobs. But, like Joe, relax and give it some thought. Your retirement may just gradually gain internal traction.

Alex retired at 55. Not being married nor having children to worry about, he focused on saving 25 percent of his salary for the last 10 years of his career. In retirement, he now travels extensively: Florence for several months, then on to France . . . then back to his New York apartment to plan his next adventure.

However, sometimes your best-laid plans can change. Consider Don's experience. He was a writer all his life. When he retired, the great American novel was his goal. To his surprise, it didn't happen. "I retired from work pressures, and once I started on the novel, I realized it was simply too much work." He then thought about his childhood and one of his loves, art. He now paints landscapes. A peaceful endeavor. Finally, to his great joy, he rediscovered his family—his wife, his children, his grandchildren.

Don, like many, needed to explore and discover his own retirement. After two years, he finally found the tranquillity his career didn't give him. When he worked, he had deadlines every week, sometimes several a day. He traveled incessantly and missed seeing his kids grow up. "I even thought about work when I did attend an occasional sporting event for my kids."

An aggressive form of prostate cancer forced him to "listen to my body." He beat the cancer, and now with dog and wife in tow, he runs two miles a day.

Don further has learned about not putting a dollar sign on every activity. "Some of my retired friends say they don't want to volunteer at the hospital or even do part-time work because it doesn't pay anything or not very much." Retirement should be a time when you can choose what you want to do, regardless of money.

Keep an Open Mind

Of all the advice retirees have given me to pass on to others, one idea stands out. They say keep an open mind. Try many things. Even try things you assume you wouldn't enjoy.

What you may find, they say from experience, are those things you think you will enjoy, well, maybe you won't actually enjoy them at all. And those things you think you wouldn't enjoy—you might find yourself actually liking them.

Like George who grudgingly played some tennis with his buddies. His interest, however, slowly grew. Now if he doesn't play tennis twice a week, he feels something important in his life is missing. Or Gladys, who never liked gardening, but started puttering around the yard. Now she is active in a local gardening club, helps in public gardening projects, and is proud of her refurbished lawn and garden.

Dorothy was single and lived in a huge Victorian house her parents left her. Before retirement, she had thought she would finally clean out the house, including the attic and garage. But she also had always dreamed of mountain climbing. So, she started visiting the Adirondacks, then the Rockies. She is currently off to New Zealand to enjoy the great vistas. Her house remains messy as ever.

Above all, look to yourself. Be determined to shuck off the useless baggage you've accumulated over the years. Think of the things you would ideally like to do. Dream of things that are difficult to do.

Learn the Computer

If there is one divide between the retired and the working, it seems to be the computer. If you haven't yet taken the plunge, then it's about time. The trick is to think of a specific task that you would like to do with the computer. This will provide the motivation for learning how to use it. Is it sending e-mail to the grandkids? Keeping track of your portfolio? Keeping the family tree updated? Or simply keeping in touch with friends and family by posting recent photos of everyone?

Exercise Your Mind

Learning, in general, is the ticket to staying mentally young. Elderhostel is an easy way to get back into education, outside of high school or local summer college courses.

Keep in Shape

No excuses now for not having enough time. With your doctor's guidance, you have plenty of options to keep an active regimen. If you've been sedentary, start by walking. Not a power walk before you're ready, just a casual stroll as a first step. The long-term goal of an appropriate exercise program is a better quality of life.

A program with a group or just with your spouse or friend, may fit your needs, or an individual activity may suit you. Local Ys or health clubs offer a variety of programs. Swimming, or just water exercise, can be an alternative to walking in cold weather.

A Lifetime of Learning

- *Elderhostel.* With no educational requirements, it allows you to get back into an educational setting for a week. Your library has all the information, or check out www.elderhostel.org.
- *Visit your library and museums.* How better to stimulate your mind than with racks of books, or a tour of a local museum?
- *Attend lectures and talks.* Meet people in the community for socialization and learning.
- *Free college courses.* Many colleges allow attendance for no credit. No tests and lots of education.
- *Take organized trips.* You can get away from your local community to plays, museums, events, discoveries.

When you combine exercise with good eating habits, you're on your way to keeping your physical body ready for your active retirement life.

A good friend, Larry Smiley, sets an admirable example. Like most executives, he was tied to a desk with little time for exercise. At retirement, he resolved to change his ways. After one year of a 5-days-a-week exercise regimen at his local health club, he has lost 21 pounds, three inches on his belt, and reduced his fat content from 34 percent to 24 percent. His key: He and his wife go to the club to start their day together, offering mutual encouragement.

Stretch Your Thinking

If you need to think more expansively about retirement, ponder these words, or others that stimulate your imagination:

adventure, spirituality, caring, family, politics, helping, relationships, solitude, reading, doing, loving, journey, sharing, play, friendships . . .

Work, Yes Work!

Today's definition of retirement can include work. Retirement actually has two definitions. The traditional one says retirement is when you no longer work. Today's definition says you don't have to work because you have enough money, but want to.

Cautions in Retirement

The transition to retirement can present problems. You've never been retired, so how would you know? There's potentially a positive, or negative, life on the other side. Consider the following cautions retirees have related to me.

Beware of bringing your career habits home with you when you retire. If you were a manager at work, guess what could happen when you retire? Managers are trained to boss people around. So, yes, you could try to manage the household, which if you are married may not be the very best strategy with your spouse. One manager decided to offer constructive criticism on how his wife was vacuuming. He ended up with the chore himself.

Another manager told me that he decided to do the cooking. "We men are better cooks, if we set our minds to it." The next day his wife woke up stunned to see her kitchen completely reorganized. The next day, however, when he woke up, his tool shed was completely reorganized. He called a truce. He realized that he and his wife both needed to make any changes with care and consultation.

The Lesson of Charlie

To keep a positive frame of mind, Charlie always said, "Never ask a retired person: 'How are you?'"

He or she, will likely proceed to actually tell you, for the next hour. "Well," she might begin, "my back has pain and I take . . . for it. I saw my doctor last week and she said . . ." And on and on.

The trick Charlie said was to always avoid the question. Try substitutes, like "The Yankees finally won a game," "Sure is a nice day," "Did you hear what's happening in Washington?"

Charlie was a positive person and realized that while physical ailments are a reality of retirement, dwelling on them doesn't make for a positive day.

Sometimes There Are Problems

On occasion, retirees tell me of the three Ds: Death, Divorce, and Depression. Death, because more and more of your friends and family do pass on. Divorce, because many couples confront their difficulties and decide to split. Depression, because people can lose their sense of meaning in life without the direction that involvement in a job or raising a family can provide.

Retirement, like life before it, surely has all of these events. But without children to raise and jobs to focus on, retirees have more time to dwell on unhappy feelings. Suggestion: Get involved with others if lonely. Get professional counseling if necessary. You've worked too hard over a lifetime not to enjoy some measure of happiness later in your life.

Be Realistic about Driving in Older Age

Leo, a car mechanic in New York City, told me how he helps older people who have difficulty driving. When an older driver comes in frequently to have car dents repaired, he sometimes has a talk with the person's kids. Often, they tell him they are concerned as well. The answer is for the parent to give up his or her driver's license. But, how to do this in a caring way?

Leo's solution: When the older person comes in, Leo points out how expensive these repairs are, along with the cost of insurance and maintenance. Why not pay a car service $120 for 20 rides, or hire a limo or per-ride car service? The older person may be more inclined to agree and give up the car, especially if the kids step in and pay for some of the expense.

A Positive Attitude

Retirement has the potential for the best of times. Your life changes from a workaday world to one of personal activities and leisure. Your experience tells you that a positive attitude can give you an outward and inward smile.

Keep a Sense of Humor

If you have a well-developed sense of humor, indulge it. If you have an average dose, amplify it. If you seem to have lost it, rekindle it. Laughter is good for the disposition. Yours and those around you.

Be creative. Stay away from these standard retirement jokes:

"I married for better or worse, but not for lunch."

"I now have twice the husband, but one-half the income."

A Personal Note

In the middle of conducting a seminar a few years ago, one of the participants waved his hand and asked me: "You're teaching us all about retirement, but what about you? What does retirement mean to you—personally?" Rarely at a loss for words, I was momentarily caught off guard. "First off," I said after a pause to collect my wits. "I don't intend to retire in the usual sense. There are so many things that I want to do in my professional life, that I'm not sure I'll have time to retire."

Retirement is my work. So retiring from retirement seems to be an oxymoron, like entering Alice's opposite looking glass. Perhaps it goes back to my freshman year in college, where 300 or so of us sat in a University of Wisconsin lecture hall. A professor offered his take on the future. He said we are becoming so economically efficient in providing all the things we need—food and manufacturing—that some day few people, if any, will actually need to work. In fact, he said, we will have to pay people not to work. This idea always intrigued me and is the core of much of our present-day retirement.

Final Bits of Life Advice

- *If you're young.* Develop discipline and positive work habits.
- *If you're in mid-career.* Renew your work life as well as your personal life.
- *If you're retired.* Think of life's possibilities.

Yes. The chase of the Big R gets you back to possibilities. Think of retirement as that point when you can do what you want, how you want, and when you want.

Appendix A

Retirement and Tax FAQs

Here are some common, and uncommon, questions I've gotten over the years, including the most recent ones about the new tax bill, the Economic Growth and Tax Relief Reconciliation Act of 2001 passed by Congress on May 26, 2001, and signed into law by President Bush on June 7.

Q. What is the bottom line of the new tax law for retirement?

A. The bottom line is that there are more ways you can now save for retirement, and you have more flexibility with respect to the various tax rules. In addition, there have been two changes to retirement planning for the better, compared with the recent past. Early in 2001, the complicated distribution rules at 70½ were simplified. Also in 2001, the Social Security earnings test at 65 (or your normal retirement age) was eliminated. Taken together, these new rules make retirement planning easier.

Some of the tax provisions are direct including increased contributions, such as for IRAs ($3,000 in 2002 and increasing in future years), and catch-up provisions for those over age 50 ($500 in 2002 and increasing in future years).

Other provisions are more indirect. Several parts of the tax bill help pay for college. For many families, retirement savings are whatever is left over after paying their kids' college bills. An increase in contributions to Education IRAs and tax-free payouts from Section 529 plans can help keep more money in parents' pockets. The contribution limits for Education IRAs have been only $500 a year, but beginning in 2002 they increase to $2,000 to an account each year for each child through age 17. This should make these IRAs more plausible for families. The more popular way to save has been to use the relatively new (1997) Section 529 college savings plans. They have caught on quickly especially because the contribution amounts are quite high, depending on the plan. Beginning in 2002 the withdrawals for college expenses will be tax free. This is no small matter and will make these plans even more popular.

Another way the tax bill helps is by decreasing income taxes for most taxpayers. Although the decreases may not be dramatic, every little bit helps families who must closely watch their expenses. Also, the child tax credit, which has been $500, will increase gradually to double by 2010. It increases to $600 in 2002, goes to $700 in 2005, $800 in 2009, and $1,000 in 2010. There are additional provisions such as a reduction of the so-called marriage penalty, and there are new rules for deducting student loan interest.

Q. Do the sunset provisions of the new tax law bother you?

A. Sure. How could they not? Provisions like the estate tax going from being eliminated in 2010 to being fully restated in 2011 are obviously troubling. Actually all the tax cuts are repealed after 2010. My guess is that there will be efforts to make the tax law permanent long before 2011, although it may not succeed until the economy is stronger with concomitant higher surpluses. There does seem to be a general consensus on both sides of the aisle that the tax law is a good one and should be preserved.

Q. Aren't the various new tax rules complicated and will test the patience of taxpayers?

A. Yes and no. Any changes in rules, laws, or taxes always frustrate taxpayers because there are better things to do than to try and understand them. It makes life, which is complicated and frustrating enough, even more so. On the other hand, the new rules and taxes will save money, which will be appreciated, and simplify planning.

Q. What do you see as biggest obstacle to retirement today and tomorrow?

A. Today, the biggest obstacle is twofold: a low savings rate and a sluggish stock market. Tomorrow, the biggest obstacle for a high percentage of people may be Social Security. Why? Because so many people depend on it to retire at all. About 50 percent of workers do not have pensions, 401(k)s, 403(b)s, or 457s. They must rely on their own savings and Social Security. But, we have an impending problem with the financial structure of both Social Security and Medicare.

Q. Why do politicians talk about the looming problems of Social Security, but don't propose to do anything about it?

A. It actually is surprising. I find no good reason why there are so few proposals for solving this problem. Unlike other problems we wrestle with as a society, we have already defined the parameters of this problem. We know how many people will be retiring over the next 20 years (because they've already been born), so actuaries have provided very accurate figures on which to base planning. In fact, we've known the size of the problem for some time.

President Bush is proposing adding personal accounts to help out. Others have proposed increasing the age to receive full benefits. While the merits of these accounts and retirement age are and should be debatable, those who disagree with these proposals refuse to offer any alternatives. For all of Washington's open rhetoric and debate, silence is not a credible answer. Although "bonds" are supposed to pay for the upcoming shortfall to the system, they are only an expressed obligation—no money has been set aside to make the bonds good. Because the amount of money is so great, it is imperative to get concrete about solutions to this problem. Perhaps the politicians are afraid to say that they will have to raise taxes or decrease benefits. But, for financial planning, it is better to know what the future benefits will be so you can plan for them.

Taxpayers should be asking their representatives what they plan to do about it. Perhaps additional prodding will give strength to the politicians.

Q. Why don't companies offer phased-in retirement?

A. They don't know how to do it. Many people would like to phase down work first to a four-day workweek, then to three days, and so forth, gradually easing into retirement. They would get to keep their foot in their organization's day-to-day activities and maintain contact with coworkers. This structure also can make the abrupt work cutoff less abrupt. But it's a difficult balancing act to effectuate. An organization needs a full-time person, if not actually expecting a person-and-a-half for each job.

The person who can generally do this best is the self-employed professional, a dentist, doctor, or psychologist who can simply see fewer patients, or an accountant, consultant, or lawyer who merely takes on fewer clients. Most others just have to work five days a week and abruptly halt it when they retire.

Q. Because we know that old age can bring physical and mental problems, what are some ideas to plan for this?

A. There are for most people two stages of retirement: Active to about 85, and deteriorating health after 85. Some retirees tell me that they want to travel for the first five years of retirement while they are still in good health. I encourage them to think in terms of being active in the first years of retirement, but I also tell them not to be surprised if they continue to be active and in good health for many years. Although this will not be true for everyone, it is true for most. Therefore, I suggest that they should plan for their expenses to continue at a level of an active life. Then, later in life when they may have to slow down, they may be spending money on other things, medical care, and help around the house. A widow in San Diego once told me, "At 75 I don't climb ladders anymore, so I have to pay someone to do it."

Q. How should I factor taxes in my investment returns?

A. We can't ignore taxes, but in most cases you have to treat the resultant investment and taxes on them separately. Say you have $10,000 in a five-year CD earning 5 percent interest, and you're in the 28 percent marginal tax bracket. Interest on CDs is taxable each year, so you'll have to pay taxes on that interest each year. However, like almost every taxpayer, you wouldn't go to your bank and take out the exact amount of interest that resulted from the CD. Not only would that be a little strange, you would probably incur a penalty if you did.

So, use the full interest rate to calculate your investments, realizing that you'll pay the taxes on them from your other pocket.

Q. I have a choice in my pension plan of an annuity or lump sum payout, but my broker says that I'd be foolish not to take the lump sum. Why?

A. Realize that brokers make their money from investing money and in this case the lump sum. They don't make money if you take the annuity. The advantages of the annuity to you are the higher regular payouts, the peace of mind that it can give you, and the fact that it will never run out. The advantages of the lump sum to you are its flexibility to take higher withdrawals and the potential to increase the lump sum through investments.

Brokers often argue for the lump sum by saying that if you die early the extra money goes back to the company or that you could leave the lump sum to your heirs. This argument seems not in the client's best interest, but rather the heirs' best interest. After working very hard over a full career to get to retirement, it seems to me people should select the best option for themselves. Or, put more directly, I generally see no need to give a priority to heirs, to make sure they get the maximum from your estate, versus what is in your own best interest.

Q. I've read somewhere that several pensions may be worth less than one?

A. This can be seen in Table A.1. Since pensions are usually based on your last salary with a company, pensions earned early in your career are based on that lower salary rather than the higher salary at your last job. Working at four different companies with typical pension plans, each with 10 years of service, could result in total pensions 40 percent less than working at one company for 40 years.

Yet, if you're lucky enough to have a pension, you could be better off with that pension than with a 401(k) plan. For *Money* magazine's May 1994 issue, I calculated an example of a person covered with a typical pension at age 35, earning $50,000, and staying with that company until age 60. There could be an eventual annual pension of $36,971, or $739,415 over an expected lifetime. But if that person instead had a typical 401(k) plan and it earned only a modest 5 percent, there would be an equivalent annual income of $30,162, or $603,238 total, 18 percent less. The lesson here is if you have a 401(k) plan, you hope for two things: your investment smarts to get a higher return and the stock market to cooperate.

Q. Why do some pension plans subtract my Social Security?

A. Because, although little known, Social Security pays more as a percentage of salary to a lower earner. A person earning a salary of $20,000 would get a Social Security benefit of about $8,100, or 40 percent of salary. A person earning

TABLE A.1 Values of Pension Plans

NUMBER OF COMPANIES	YEARS AT EACH	TOTAL AMOUNT OF PENSIONS	PERCENTAGE DECREASE
1	40	$48,000	
2	20	35,000	27
3	13.3	30,700	36
4	10	29,000	40

$65,000 would get about $15,300, or 24 percent of salary. The tilting, or skewing, of Social Security benefits toward the lower earner makes the reasonable assumption that the lower earner probably doesn't have many other retirement resources, like pensions.

Given this tilting, companies in turn are allowed to pay higher pensions to higher paid workers to offset this imbalance. Doing so then allows for the equalization of percentage of retirement benefits for everyone. To create this equalization, actuaries have devised what are called Social Security "offset" formulas that involve subtraction of up to one-half of your Social Security.

Q. Why is it hard to estimate a pension?

A. Because their formulas are often too complicated. Pensions vary by company, so if you think you know one plan, another could mystify you.

Here is an example of a typical pension formula:

Annual Pension equals *1 percent* times *years of service* times *average final salary*

Usually there are three things that are multiplied together: a percentage, the number of years you've worked for the company, and the average of your last three or five years' salary. Using our simple formula, let's say you are 65 years old and ready to retire. Let's further say you have 20 years of service and your average salary is calculated at $50,000. Our typical pension plan would then calculate to be:

Annual Pension equals *0.01* times *20* times *$50,000*

Annual Pension equals *$10,000* a year.

This means you would receive a pension equal to $10,000 a year beginning at age 65 for as long as you live. You might observe that multiplying the first two numbers together, the percentage times years of service, gives a percentage of your last salary. In this example, one percentage point times 20 years results in 20 percent. Thus, the pension is calculated as 20 percent of your last salary.

You can see why these plans are technically called *defined benefit plans.* The benefit is "defined" by the three parameters. If you had more years of service or earned more money, your pension would be greater. For the moment, we'll skip the complications if you're married, if you take it earlier than age 65, or if it is offered as a lump sum.

You can begin to see how difficult it is to project this type of benefit. If you're 45, say, you don't know how long you'll stay at your company, and what your salary will be 15 to 20 years hence. To be sure, your 401(k) plan is also difficult to project. You need to estimate how much you and your company will contribute and what the investment rate of return will be. However, projecting your current 401(k) balance seems more straightforward.

Q. What is an accrued benefit?

A. Companies that have a pension plan usually provide an annual pension estimate for you called *an accrued benefit,* which is little understood and not always much help, unless you are near retirement. One of my 40-something clients had an accrued benefit as of December 31, 1997, of $467 a month. This means that if she left her company at the end of 1997, at age 65 she would receive a pension of $467 a month. She has "accrued" this benefit payable at her retirement. Another client is 64, has an accrued benefit of $1,373 a month and plans to retire next year. His actual retirement benefit will only be a tad higher, given just one more year of service and only a slightly higher salary.

Q. How can I estimate my own pension with these complicated formulas?

A. Here's a generalized way to do so. Keep in mind, however, unless you're an actuary, you won't be able to do a precise calculation. The trick to calculating an estimate is to first look for an example of a pension calculation in your pension booklet. (If you don't have such a booklet, gently remind your benefits manager that it's required by law.) Second, by trial and error, find a simple formula to get the same result. Here's an example I found in one of my client's booklets:

> *Pension booklet example.* An employee who has 20 years of service and a final salary of $60,000, would receive an estimated annual pension of *$13,200.*

Since almost all formulas use the number of years of service and an average of your final salary, it's a matter of finding a generalized formula that gets to the $13,200, even though the formula may have a Social Security offset.

By trial and error, I found the percentage in the formula to be:

1.1 percent times *Years of service* times *Average final salary*

In our example, this works out to be:

Estimated pension equals *0.011 × 20 × $60,000*
Estimated pension equals *$13,200* a year

So, we've estimated the age 65 benefit if the person stayed with this employer and was averaging $60,000 at retirement. Emphasis here on *estimate*.

Q. Didn't you calculate somewhere a generalized pension formula?

A. Yes, I constructed Table A.2 using a 1 percent pension formula.

Q. What is the meaning of the term *404(c)?*

A. It's a provision that allows a company to provide investment education, not advice, to its employees. There were regulations under the main laws governing pension plans (called ERISA for short) that prohibited such information, but there was a realization in recent years that it was generally in the best interest of employees to receive such education as long as it was done impartially.

Q. How do you define *traditional retirement?*

A. Traditional retirement is being able to retire at 65 or before.

Q. What is an alternative retirement career?

A. It's a creative career choice later in life when you have tired of your regular career. Because many people will either have to work or simply want to, moving to a career that one finds exciting can bring personal as well as financial rewards.

Q. Will there be some people who won't be able to afford retirement at all?

A. There are actually a number of people in their 70s and 80s who can't afford retirement now. They don't get any publicity so they are the unseen segment of retirement. Social Security is the one program that keeps these people solvent.

TABLE A.2 Yearly Pension Estimates at Age 65 Using a 1 Percent Pension Formula

FINAL AVERAGE SALARY	YEARS OF SERVICE			
	5	10	15	20
$15,000	$ 750	$1,500	$ 2,250	$ 3,000
20,000	1,000	2,000	3,000	4,000
30,000	1,500	3,000	4,500	6,000
40,000	2,000	4,000	6,000	8,000
50,000	2,500	5,000	7,500	10,000
75,000	3,750	7,500	11,250	15,000

TABLE A.3 Percentage of People Retiring in Each Scenario

	YEAR		
	2010	2025	2050
Scenario I (traditional)	90%	50%	10%
Scenario II (alternative)	5	20	50
Scenario III (delayed retirement to age 70 or later)	5	30	40

Q. Do you think retirement will be delayed for many baby boomers?

A. Yes. I think many boomers and GenXers will find retiring at age 70 or later more and more common.

Q. Didn't you once offer a prediction of how many people would actually retire under the three scenarios of traditional, alternative retirement, and no retirement?

A. Yes, I called them the three scenarios of future retirement. I think this could play out over the next 50 years as shown in Table A.3.

Q. What is the role of work in retirement?

A. Although it seems a contradiction in terms, work is more and more a part of retirement.

One of my clients said to me recently, "I know at 70 most people think I should be retired, but I enjoy my job, which is highly technical. All the experienced people at my company have retired, and my firm needs my expertise. In fact after I retired at 65, I went to work for an engineering consulting firm that, by coincidence, contracted work with my old company. For three years then, I worked for my old firm through this consulting firm. Now my firm has hired me back on what they call a non-regular employee, whatever that means. Also, my wife doesn't want me home, so working keeps us both happy."

Fanny, age 67, says that her house became an empty, scary place to live in. Her husband, Peter, was traveling extensively and her kids moved out of the house for college or careers. The house became so "empty" that she almost couldn't bear to stay in it. Work for her was an answer.

Bob, a Chicagoan, was a chemist for a textile company for 30 years and loved his work. But when he retired at age 60, he took an unlikely position as a special van driver for a bank. His job is to carry valuable securities from one bank to another. He gets to know all the key bank officers and often gets to chat with them. He loves this job, too. At age 65, he says he wants to keep working. As a chemist, he was cooped up. Now he is able to meet and talk to people, something he longed to do.

But not all people have positive feelings about mixing work and retirement. Harold, a 65-year-old retired man, sought me out not long ago explaining that he had just lost a significant amount of money in investments and was looking for ways to deal with the realities of his new financial situation. After reviewing the details of his finances, I said to him, "One of your options is to go back to work." He looked at me, and at his wife who was sitting next to him, in disbelief. "I'm retired, I can't go back to work. That's out of the question."

Perhaps Harold, as well as many others, should remember that work is not only a basic human activity, it is something we should hold in high esteem. Perhaps we need the Amish farmers to remind us of what they have found to be a universal truth, "Work is the dignity of humankind."

Visiting Disney World recently, I noticed that about half of the attendants at rides and in the numerous gift shops had gray hair. People at older ages were thriving at our country's biggest resort. If you look around, you will see older people working at all kind of jobs. As one manager of a New Jersey Shore restaurant said, "Why shouldn't I hire them? They are of a generation that appreciates a job, they get here on time, and they are extremely responsible."

Then, again, midcareer people are searching and sometimes finding a better career. Like the researcher for a major pharmaceutical company who is starting over as a high school math teacher because she says it's really her. Like the architect who is starting a import textile business. Like the banker who is growing organic vegetables. The word *career* doesn't even seem accurate. *Lifework* fits better. It is earning a living doing something that you want to do and having a rewarding workday. It's almost like not working at all.

Alternative careers may be the baby boomer answer to a midlife crisis. It's more than a different career, it is more than just being self-employed. It is you. In the middle of your life when the pressures of a job you don't particularly like get to you, you covet a job and corresponding personal life that is more satisfying to you and your family.

We are shuttled into careers and onto paths we often haven't planned for and in some cases wish we didn't have to do. Alternative careers are those work activities we have chosen specifically to do because they are meaningful to us.

This can happen at midlife because by then we know ourselves well enough to select what we would like to do for the rest of our lives.

Or, it could happen in retirement itself.

Q.   What is the most basic advice you give to retirees?

A.   Make the most of retirement, as hopefully you have done with the earlier years of your life.

Appendix B
Econ 301: Some Thorny Economic Issues

People are focusing on several advanced economic questions: Will our current economic slowdown reverse itself in short order? Why do we have a strong dollar and why does it matter? What are some of the personal implications of globalization? How will the economics of an older population play out? Why is there such a noisy debate about Social Security and Medicare trust funds? Just how could the boomer lament, "My kids will not have it as good as I have had it" play out?

Q. Will our current economic slowdown reverse itself in short order?

A. Although we like the extended business cycle that monetary policy seems to have given us, we don't seem to like the longer, albeit shallower, slowdowns and the length of time it takes after a slowdown to get the economy going again. Perhaps this can be called the *monetary business cycle.* The old cycle took 4 to 5 years to play out from growth to recession: the new cycle has doubled and is 8 to 10 years.

Everything is more controlled by the Fed—interest rates, inflation, economic growth, stock market growth (with the exception of the technology and Internet bubble of 1995 through 1999).

If this is true, then we'll have to live with a longer slowdown than the standard cycle of the past. The first monetary slowdown occurred in 1990 after 8 years of growth from 1982. The slowdown was prolonged, followed by a painful but steady recovery. It may be a model we'll have to live with. This means that investors will become quite frustrated as they wait impatiently for their portfolios to recover.

What to do? Take the long view, set up your portfolio with a long-term asset allocation and resolve to add patience to your mind-set.

Q. Why do we have a strong dollar and why does it matter?

A. As we close out the summer of 2001, we are still buying more goods from Europe and Asia than they in turn buy from us, but the dollar remains high. Why? Classical economics tells us when a country buys more goods from abroad, its currency should decline. A trading partner wants its own currency (Chinese can't buy a cup of coffee in China with dollars) and thus exchanges the dollars it gets from us and converts them back to its own currency. The more we buy, the more dollars China has to convert. Thus, dollars become plentiful and should drop in value. Simple supply and demand.

But the dollar has remained strong. I just returned from Paris where the dollar can buy 7.5 francs. Two years ago, one dollar could only fetch 6.3 francs. It makes buying croissants cheaper along Rue Cler, but it also leaves U.S. companies with less profits as they have to repatriate francs back into dollars.

Alan Greenspan has long offered the answer. He has repeatedly said that foreigners like the stability of our investments and continue to invest here. Thus, foreign money flowing into our country for investments has offset the trade deficit that flows money out of the country. And until foreigners lose interest in our investments, the dollar will tend to remain strong.

This also has a direct effect on our international portfolios. If you invest in a mutual fund of foreign companies, a strong dollar would decrease your profits. An American investor not only would like foreign stocks to do well, the investor also hopes that the dollar weakens so the profits are magnified positively. Yes, croissants are cheaper in Paris when the dollar is strong, but stock prices are amplified for an American investor when the dollar is weak.

The bottom line for U.S. international investors: Expect your international stock funds to disappoint until foreign economies perk up and the dollar weakens.

Q. What are some of the personal implications of globalization?

A. It's not news that the world is becoming one big marketing-labor pool. We've moved beyond the global village and are becoming the global metropolis. Disparate global parts are being connected with amazing speed. Through CNN and the Internet, we are seeing the emergence of one global advertising net.

What has this wrought? A more impersonal world. Although we seem closer together when we watch the Weather Channel's European or Asian forecast, the lines of communications get longer. We become smaller fish in a bigger world.

As part of this larger world, we are also forced to take more individual responsibility because no one seems to be doing it for us. We have the task of managing complex investments in 401(k)s as companies distance themselves from pensions, which they took the responsibility for investing.

Perhaps it is not unreasonable that many are uneasy because of these changes and uncertainties. Our new century ushers in this dichotomy with the seemingly contradictory movements of increasing global influence that shrinks the world and newfound individual responsibility that must deal with an impersonal world.

We might want to harken back to a time when life was more personal and less complicated like the agrarian life of the Amish. Although few of us would opt to return to this farming life, it has qualities that many of us may yearn for.

As Compton's 1996 Online Encyclopedia (see Farming) says:

> For many the lure of farming lies in some of the conditions that it offers, such as continuity, order, and regularity. It provides a measured pace of life with clear goals and a tangible finished product, usually food. There is a sense of fulfillment and productivity in doing something regarded as important. Family members work together with clear objectives. There is a feeling of order and completion as the year unfolds in a close association with nature. Obstacles are visible, problems are clearer, and the means to overcome them seem close at hand.

For retirement, the Amish father hands over the farm to a son; then Dad and Mom move to an extension off the main house and, for the rest of their lives, settle down to various work ventures—carpentry, woodworking, furniture making, sewing, weaving, canning. If people need care in their old age, the younger Amish family members tend to them—although they use doctors, medicines, and hospitals when needed. But there are no nursing homes, no retirement villages. And for the strong, there is no time for retirement, even though their life expectancy is as long as ours.

Through this living museum of the Amish, we can see close family and community ties providing stability throughout people's lives. In our industrial past, that stability was eventually shifted to a safety net of Social Security and long company careers providing company pensions. It also helped that the Depression instilled a solid savings ethic to put money away for a rainy day when our economy finally gained strength after World War II.

That safety net, of necessity, is now shifting to ourselves, to our individual resources. We can no longer count on organizations to take care of us. Even marriages are no longer certain, which provides more uncertainty as financial resources get divided. Whether in our careers or our personal lives, we will be more dependent on our individual resources—finances, career, and a network of friends and shrinking families.

Within the context of the global metropolis, there is uncertainty where jobs, careers, and retirement are headed. But, the growing dependence on ourselves and our careers may force us to rethink and rededicate ourselves to our current line of work. We might even want to take advanced courses or graduate programs to add depth to what we are doing. Or we might even decide now is the time to start a business that we could enjoy well into our later years. This rethinking could lead to a more satisfying career, especially in the second half of life.

It may also force us to better balance work, family, leisure, education, and community service. Personal renewal of skills and abilities could be at the heart of this rethinking. Perhaps that is the message from the global metropolis: You get to be more individual in what you do and how you do it, but you also get the concomitant personal responsibility.

Q. How will the economics of an older population play out?

A. About 35 percent of our federal budget goes for Social Security and Medicare. With the baby boomers soon to retire, that figure will inevitably inch upward. But perhaps that's about right.

Older people are a larger and larger portion of our population. The Census Bureau reports that the 85-and-over crowd increased by 38 percent in the past decade. The over-65 population will double over the next 30 years.

Occasionally, there have been stories about how the younger generation will rebel against the older generation because too much is being spent on the older cohort. AARP's membership (50 and older) is about 33 million strong, almost half of that population.

This gives the older generation political clout. But younger generations have a direct stake in the older generations—it represents their parents, aunts, and uncles. Thus, don't look for generational warfare anytime soon.

Q. Why is there such a noisy debate about trust funds?

A. The rhetoric is hot because the very fabric of political beliefs is at stake. The Democrats do not want a discussion of any changes now, and the Republicans want to propose changes to deal with the future shortfall sooner than later. Why? Since Social Security is the cornerstone of Democratic programs, they understandably want to avoid proposing any changes at this time. They fear that giving in to the discussion of any future tax increases or benefit cutbacks would prompt a full assault on Social Security itself. The Republicans, ever practical, want to propose needed changes now so as to put Social Security's house in order for the long haul.

But the rhetoric gets confusing. Let's consider the trust funds of Social Security and Medicare and see how arguments get struck.

Social Security has a trust fund composed of special government bonds to secure its payments. It was put in place so future congresses and presidents would make good on the promise to pay benefits under the current formulas. However, it was never specified where money would come from when they had to cash the bonds in or, if you will, meet the commitments made to the current system. Since everyone wants their benefits, politicians seem on the right side of the people's wishes.

The first problem will come about year 2015. That's when it's projected that there will not be enough money from payroll taxes to pay for all the benefits. Cashing in the bonds, or even paying their hypothetical interest will simply mean finding general revenues to pay for the shortfall. The first several years of shortfall will probably not be a great burden if we are still running a budget surplus. In other words, we'll find the money for the first several years. But, as years roll on, there will be greater and greater shortfalls and a greater need to do something permanent about it.

One solution will be to simply add to debt. (That's one reason to pay down debt now—so it will be at a low enough level and won't cause too much of a fiscal problem.) Another will be to cut back on benefits or to increase taxes, but that will have to wait until later.

The Medicare trust fund is even more complicated. As many people know, there are Parts A and B to Medicare. But few people know that there is only a trust fund for Part A, the hospital part. The money comes from 1.45 percent of the total 7.65 percent payroll taxes, and in fact has no income limit as do the retirement and disability parts. Part B, which pays doctor bills, has no trust fund. It is funded one-fourth by those retired ($50 per retiree per month in 2001) and three-fourths by general revenue (approximately $65 billion a year).

One side of the political aisle says that the Medicare trust fund is balanced; the other side says that the claim ignores Part B, which has an unfunded annual shortfall of $65 billion a year. As these issues come to the fore, you'll perhaps be better armed with the preceding trust fund semantics to argue whichever side you feel strongly about.

Q. Just how could the boomer lament, "My kids will not have it as good as I have had it" play out?

A. The baby boom generation has striven for several decades to gain the economic good life and has largely succeeded. Boomers have worked hard as well as smart. But a lament is heard. The American unwritten way is for each generation to climb the shoulders of the previous one and do better. It seems now that boomer children are struggling, and will continue to struggle, to attain this escalation of a better life. Boomers have concluded that their progeny will simply have to do with less.

The author questions this narrow definition of what is a better life. Boomer life experience has largely been shaped by material goods. After World War II, we built the greatest economic and consumer giant known to humankind. We were able to provide the most materialistic life ever imagined. We have at the moment probably overreached our ability to give ourselves more electronics, more cars, more houses, more luxuries.

But who says materialism is the end of all ends? Is providing more and more goods the end of our human development? Perhaps our current comfortable materialism can now give us the opportunity to move to another level. Although it could take many directions, it could focus inward toward a more spiritual life, or outward to our role in society including giving back to society. It could be a personal effort to create more balance between work and personal life, or an effort to concentrate on a few long-ignored aspects of one's life.

Whatever it could be, it could result in a more satisfying, deeper life, as opposed to the simple accumulation of more material goods. Boomers could strive to pass on to their children this idea of providing a better life than solely the material life. How the boomers deal with this challenge as a group could largely determine their place in history and their personal satisfaction and contentedness at the end of their lives.

Glossary

Actuary A person who calculates risks and mortality, giving us life expectancy tables.

ADR or American Depository Receipt A certificate issued by a foreign company that is traded on a U.S. stock exchange.

Annuity A standard form of pension payout, a monthly payment in retirement for life.

Bear market A stock market characterized by falling stock prices.

Beneficiary The person named in an IRA, 401(k), or insurance policy who will receive the value of the plan or policy.

Bond An investment in an interest-bearing security offered by companies.

Book value The value of a company arrived at by dividing the equity of a company (assets minus liabilities) by the number of outstanding shares of a company.

Bull market A stock market characterized by increasing stock prices.

Business cycle A recurring ebb and flow of business activity. Traditionally, there are four parts to the cycle: expansion, prosperity, contraction, and recession.

Buyout An offer by a company to provide additional money if an employee will accept termination or retirement.

Cap or Capitalization Refers to the total value of a company's stock. It is determined by multiplying the value of one share of stock by the number of shares available to be sold, or outstanding.

Capital gain The special tax given to stocks, mutual funds, and other assets sold if held long enough. Currently, an asset held for a year and a day is called a long-term capital gain (or loss) and is taxed at 20 percent. If in the lowest tax bracket, the long-term capital gain is 10 percent. An asset held for a shorter period is regular income (or loss).

Cash An investment in a money market fund or similar short-term and stable value of principal. It is often a holding investment while an investor decides how to invest in the stock market.

Cash balance pension plan   A retirement plan that shows a "balance" or the amount in the account each year. Usually the employer contributes all the money to the plan.

CD (certificate of deposit)   An investment usually offered by a bank in an interest-bearing account.

Closed-end mutual fund   A mutual fund that offers a limited number of shares. They are then traded as is, without redemption or addition of shares. This is in contrast to the common mutual fund that issues unlimited shares. As investors want more shares, a common mutual fund issues more shares. As investors redeem shares, the common mutual fund buys them back.

COBRA   The law that allows a leaving employee to be covered under the employer's medical plan, generally for up to 18 months. The employee will be charged roughly the rate of the employer's cost.

Commission   A fee charged by a broker or financial planner to sell an investment or insurance product, usually as a percentage of the investment.

Cost basis   The original cost of an asset. It is used to determine the capital gain (or loss) when that asset is sold.

CPI (consumer price index)   The monthly measure of price movements issued by the Bureau of Labor Statistics. The Bureau frequently samples the prices of products in various stores around the country.

Defined benefit plan   A pension plan where there is a formula for a retirement benefit; for example, the formula might define a benefit as 1 percent of final salary times years of employment service.

Defined contribution plan   A savings plan where the contribution is defined, for example, that you can contribute up to 10 percent of your salary to the plan. The final benefit at retirement is undefined; in this case, it is whatever is in the plan at that time.

Diversification   The strategy of having a variety of investments, stocks, bonds, and money market funds in a portfolio.

Dividend   A payment, usually quarterly, of company earnings.

Dow Jones Industrial Average   An index of the price of 30 major industrial stocks. It's calculated by formula, not simply adding up the price of each stock. There is also the Dow Jones Transportation Average, which includes 20 airline, trucking, and railroad firms. The Dow Jones Utility Average is composed of 15 gas, electric, and power companies. The three averages form the Dow Jones 65 Composite Average.

Durable power of attorney   A more recent form of a power of attorney that allows its use while a person is incapacitated.

EAFE   The Morgan Stanley index of international companies. It is commonly used as an index for international mutual funds. It stands for Europe, Australasia, and the Far East.

Earned income   Salary and net self-employment income. This is in contrast to interest, dividends, and capital gains.

Educational IRA   A way to save for college costs. No tax deduction is allowed, but the money grows tax deferred, and the withdrawals are tax-free if for allowed college expenses.

Emerging markets   The category of smaller but growing economies around the world.

ERISA   The legislation that regulates pension plans.

ESOP   A benefit plan that comprises of only company stock.

Estate planning   The planning surrounding the transferring of assets at one's death. It includes wills, trusts, and naming of beneficiaries.

Equity   A term usually referring to what you own, such as a stock or that portion of your house or condo not owned by your bank.

Executor   The person named in a will to administer the estate of a deceased person.

Exchange rate   How much of one currency can be exchanged for another.

Fed or Federal Reserve   The agency that controls the banks and monetary policy in this country.

Fiduciary   The responsibility of managing assets for someone or some institution. It also specifies the standard of acting in the best interest of that person or institution.

Fiscal policy   The policy of a government to use budget surpluses or deficits to stimulate the economy. This is in contrast to monetary policy where the Federal Reserve tries to regulate interest rates to stimulate or cool down the economy.

529 College Tuition plan   A plan prescribed by a state that allows for after-tax contributions, tax deferred investments and, under the new tax law, tax-free withdrawals.

401(k) plan   The popular savings plan at companies. The main feature is the before-tax contributions, namely; one's salary is not taxed before it's contributed. Companies usually contribute a portion to an employee's account.

403(b) plan   A popular savings plan for hospital and nonprofit organizations. The main feature is the before-tax contributions.

457 plan   A popular savings plan at municipalities. It's actually a form of deferred compensation, but like 401(k)s and 403(b)s, it offers before-tax contributions.

Fundamental analysis   One of two approaches in analyzing the stock market or individual stocks—the other is technical analysis. Fundamental analysis uses business earnings and economic activity to determine how a particular company or market may do. Technical analysis uses market volume and price movements to determine how a particular company or market may do.

Future value   A mathematical calculation of a value of an investment, or any value, sometime in the future. For example, the value of $1,000 invested at 7 percent for 10 years equals a future value of $2,000.

Growth stocks   Stocks that have a higher P/E ratio or book value than average. This is in contrast to value stocks.

Health-care proxy   A legal document designating what medical procedures to do or not do when a person becomes seriously ill.

Hedge   An investment taken to offset a possible downturn in another investment.

Hedge fund   An investment fund that is not restricted in what it can invest in. Usually any investment strategy is allowed, such as buying puts and calls, currency swaps, as well as stocks in domestic and international companies, and junk bonds. It is thought that this flexibility will provide a greater return, but at times it actually results in lower returns, given the higher risk of the investments.

Incentive stock option or ISO   A stock option that can offer a lower capital gains tax if you hold the exercised option over a year and sell the stock after two years from offering. The other form of an option is called a non-qualified stock option.

Income in respect of a decedent (IRD)   Income that would have been taxed if taken by the deceased taxpayer and will be taxed when taken by the beneficiary.

Index fund   A mutual fund that matches a specific index, like the S&P 500 or Russell 2000.

Inflation   A general rise in prices.

Insider trading   An illegal use of secret company information in buying or selling stock. It can also refer to the legal buying and selling of a stock by senior officers of a company.

Investment club   A group of investors who pool their money and decide jointly which stocks to buy and sell.

IPO or initial public offering   The first issuance of a stock to the public. It is thought that IPOs always do well, but in fact many do poorly.

IRA or Individual Retirement Account   A popular account for saving for retirement. Starting in 2002, a worker can contribute up to $3,000 a year, with an additional $500 if 50 or older.

Junk bonds   Bonds that are poorly rated. Often referred to as high-yield bonds because the requirement of having to pay higher interest for the higher risk to investors.

Keogh plan   A retirement plan for the self-employed. There are several forms including profit-sharing and money purchase plans.

Large cap   A stock that is one of the largest in the United States.

Limited partnership A form of investment where a general partner makes the decisions and limited partners share in its profits or losses. Commonly, these investments have been in oil and gas exploration, equipment leasing, and real estate.

Limit order Instructions to a broker to buy if a stock falls below a specific price or sell if a stock rises above a specific price.

Liquidity The ability of an investment to be turned into cash.

Load A commission for selling mutual funds. There are no-load, low-load, front- and back-end load mutual funds.

Long-term care insurance Insurance that covers a portion of nursing home facilities or similar care at home.

Marginal tax rate The highest tax percentage or bracket that your income is taxed for the year.

Margin call A demand by a broker for an investor, who has taken out a loan, to add to his or her account because the investor's investments have fallen in value.

Market order An order by an investor for a broker to buy a stock at the best available price or its current price.

Medicare A universal medical plan for retirees. Part A pays for hospitalization, and Part B pays for doctor bills.

Monetary policy The policy of the Federal Reserve to regulate interest rates to stimulate or cool down the economy. This is in contrast to fiscal policy where a government uses budget surpluses or deficits to stimulate the economy.

Money market fund A mutual fund of short-term interest investments. It is also called cash because it is considered to be as good as cash.

Money supply The total of a person's money in savings, CDs, money market funds, and checking accounts.

Municipal bond A bond issued by a city, state, or local government agency that usually provides a favorable tax on the interest to an investor.

Mutual fund An investment managed by an investment organization. The fund comprises specific stocks, bonds, or money market investments. The prospectus indicates the particular investments the fund is allowed to make and cannot make. A mutual fund commonly offers unlimited shares for investors to buy more or to redeem as investors want to sell. This is in contrast to a closed-end mutual fund that only offers a fixed number of shares.

Net asset value The price of one share of mutual fund. It is the value of the investments in the mutual fund divided by the number of fund shares.

No-load mutual fund   A mutual fund that has no sales charges to buy into or sell out of. It uses an 800-number and literature to sell its shares versus a sales force who will receive commissions for selling.

Nonqualified plan   A tax term referring to a retirement plan that does not provide certain tax advantages.

Nonqualified stock option or NQSO   A stock option that requires an immediate tax of ordinary income at the exercise of the option. The other form of an option is called an incentive stock option or ISO.

Nursing home   A residence for a person who can no longer take care of him- or herself.

Option   A term referring either to a stock option offered by a company to its employees or to calls and puts on stock by a broker.

Over the counter or OTC   A network of brokers who trade smaller stock, usually referring to the NASDAQ. However some larger companies decide to be traded on this network because the reporting requirements are less stringent.

Penny stocks   Inexpensive stock, often selling for less than a dollar a share.

Pension Plan   A retirement plan that pays a monthly payment to a retiree.

Per-share earnings   The earnings of one share of stock. It is the total earnings divided by the number of outstanding shares of the company.

Portfolio   The total investments of an investor.

Preferred stock   A form of stock offered by a company that pays a fixed and usually higher dividend.

Present value   A mathematical calculation of a value in today's dollars, or now. For example, the present value of $2,000 10 years from now that could earn 7% is $1,000.

Price-earnings ratio or P/E   The price of a stock divided by the amount of earnings for one share. It indicates the amount of earnings for each share and is compared to other companies in the same business sector.

Prime interest rate   The most favorable interest rate banks offer its best commercial customers.

Probate   The process of proving the validity of a will and giving authority to distribute assets in an estate.

Profit-sharing plan   A retirement plan that bases its contributions on how much money, or profits, an employer makes.

Qualified plan   A benefit plan that is generally covered by ERISA.

Real return   A return calculated minus inflation. If an investment returned 8 percent and inflation was 3 percent, the real return would be 5 percent.

Replacement ratio   A calculation of how much retirement income is needed compared with what a person earned while working; 65 percent is a common percentage.

In other words, if a person earned $50,000 while working, he or she would in general need 65 percent of that, or about $32,500 in retirement income to maintain his or her lifestyle.

Retirement That point when a person has enough money and no longer needs to work. This can also be called financial independence. The traditional definition of retirement is that point when a person has enough money and stops working.

Return Usually refers to the interest or dividend provided by an investment. The term "total return" refers to the combination of interest and gains (or losses) of an investment.

Reverse mortgage The opposite of a regular mortgage: You receive money from a bank and don't have to pay it back until you sell your house.

Rollover IRA Money that is deposited in an IRA from a pension plan, 401(k), or 403(b) plan.

Roth IRA A form of an IRA with after-tax contributions and tax-free withdrawals if held five years and over age 59½.

Russell 2000 Consists of smaller capitalization stocks and is a subset of the larger Russell 3000, which is an index of the largest publicly held companies.

S&P 500 The largest 500 domestic companies based on capitalization. The capitalization of the S&P 500 is about 70 percent of the stock market (New York, American, and NASDAQ). The S&P 500 comprises 400 industrials, 40 utilities, 40 financial, and 20 transportation companies.

SEP-IRA A specific IRA allowed for small businesses.

SIMPLE-IRA A specific IRA allowed for small businesses.

Skilled nursing facility Medicare-approved facility for the temporary care of an individual who needs nursing care and usually rehabilitation care, often when released from a hospital.

Small cap A stock that is one of the smallest in the United States.

Social Security The universal retirement plan for workers in the U.S. It was inaugurated by Franklin D. Roosevelt in 1935.

Stock An ownership in a company by a certificate.

Stock split The act of dividing the price of a stock by offering more stock. Usually a company splits two to one, meaning offering twice as many shares, which will be valued at one half the value. A company will usually split the stock if the price gets too high.

Technical analysis One of two approaches in analyzing the stock market or individual stocks—the other is fundamental analysis. Technical analysis uses market volume and price movements to determine how a particular company or market may do. Fundamental analysis uses business earnings and economic activity to determine how a particular company or market may do.

Term insurance   A life insurance policy that has no investment value, just life insurance. This is in contrast to whole life insurance that has investment values besides life insurance.

Total return   Usually refers to the combination of interest and gains (or losses) of an investment. The term *return* usually refers just to the interest or dividend provided by an investment.

Treasury securities   Bills, notes, and bonds offered by the federal government. Maturity can range from 3 months to 30 years.

Unearned income   Income from interest, dividends, or capital gains. This is in contrast to salary and net self-employment income, which are called earned income.

Value   Stock that has a lower P/E ratio or book value than average. This is in contrast to growth stock.

Vested   The value in your 401(k) or other plan that is yours if you leave.

Zero coupon bond   A bond that pays no interest but eventually pays a higher principal.

Index

A

Accrued benefit, 55, 187
Actuarial reduction, 56
After-tax contributions, 65
Age discrimination, 109–111
Age 55/59½ rule confusion, 67, 141
Alternative career, 188
Amish, 195–196
AMT (alternative minimum tax), 68
Asset Allocation:
    definition, 24, 26
    ideal, 36–37
    ideal for retirement, 150
    types, 27

B

Baby boom generation, 117, 198–199
Balanced fund, 150–151
Beneficiary, 163
Benefits, evaluating, 67
Bonds:
    basics, 31
    duration, 32
    fundamental theorem, 31
    funds versus individual bonds,
      31
    index, 29
    staggered ladder of maturities,
      25, 31–32, 152–153
Business cycle, 193–194
Buyout, 69–70
Bypass trust, 163–164

C

Capital gains tax, 38–39
Capitalization, 28
Career:
    alternative, 188
    cycle, 62
    definition, 61–62
    85/15 percent problem, 62
    personal career week, 64
    Plan X, 63
Cash balance plans, 56, 139
COBRA, 131
Community property, 165
Conduit IRA, 66

About the Author

Paul Westbrook, CFP, is President of Westbrook Financial Advisers in Ridgewood, New Jersey, and New Canaan, Connecticut, and is one of the top retirement planners in the country.

He has worked in several major corporations, a leading benefits consulting firm, and is currently head of his own firm.

Paul frequently speaks at financial planning conferences, is often quoted in such magazines as *Money* and *Fortune,* and occasionally appears on CNBC. He has written three books for Random House: *Math Smart for Business* (1997), *Word Smart for Business* (1997), and *Business Companion* (2001) (in Spanish, German, and Chinese).